Meanings into Words
Upper-Intermediate

Teacher's Book

Meanings into Words
Upper-Intermediate

An integrated course for
students of English

Teacher's Book

*Adrian Doff, Christopher Jones
and Keith Mitchell*

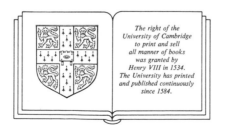

The right of the
University of Cambridge
to print and sell
all manner of books
was granted by
Henry VIII in 1534.
The University has printed
and published continuously
since 1584.

Cambridge University Press
Cambridge
London   New York   New Rochelle
Melbourne   Sydney

Published by the Press Syndicate of the University of Cambridge
The Pitt Building, Trumpington Street, Cambridge CB2 1RP
32 East 57th Street, New York, NY 10022, USA
296 Beaconsfield Parade, Middle Park, Melbourne 3206, Australia

© Cambridge University Press 1984

First published 1984

Printed in Great Britain
at the University Press, Cambridge

ISBN 0 521 28706 5 Teacher's Book
ISBN 0 521 28705 7 Student's Book
ISBN 0 521 28707 3 Workbook
ISBN 0 521 28708 1 Test Book
ISBN 0 521 24464 1 Cassette (Student's Book)
ISBN 0 521 24465 X Cassette (Drills)

MX

Contents

Contents

Part 1: Contents and organisation

1.1 Meanings into Words

Meanings into Words is an integrated course in general English which takes
students from intermediate level to the level of the Cambridge First Certificate
examination. It is divided into two parts: an *Intermediate Course* and an
Upper-Intermediate Course. The two parts can either be used together as a
single continuous course, or separately as two independent courses.

The *Intermediate Course* contains 24 units and provides material for 100–
130 classroom hours.

The *Upper-Intermediate Course* contains 15 units and provides material for
80–100 classroom hours.

At each level, in addition to the Teacher's Book, *Meanings into Words*
consists of:
Student's Book
Workbook
Test Book
Cassette (Student's Book)
Cassette (Drills)

1.2 The Upper-Intermediate Course

The Student's Book

The Student's Book contains 15 units, each providing between five and six
classroom hours, plus a final revision unit.

Each unit contains presentation and practice material, free oral practice and
writing activities, and an extended piece of either reading or listening.

At the end of each unit there is a Language Summary, which lists the main
language points covered in the unit.

Every unit is followed by an Activities page, which contains two or three
free activities. These activities combine and recycle language learned in earlier
units and in the Intermediate Course.

The Workbook

The Workbook contains homework exercises which provide extra written
practice of the main language points taught in the Student's Book. Each
Workbook unit contains four or five exercises, usually including a guided
composition.

Every five units there is a Revision Crossword.

The Test Book

The Test Book contains five short Progress Tests (45–50 minutes each) and one longer Final Achievement Test (100 minutes).

The Progress Tests occur after every three units, and test only the language of those three units. The Final Achievement Test deals with all the main language points covered in the course.

The Drills

To be used in the language laboratory, the Drills give intensive manipulation practice of key structures introduced in the units.

The Drills are divided into five Lab Sessions, occurring every three units. Each Lab Session consists of five or six drills, and lasts between 45 and 60 minutes, but it is also possible to subdivide each one into shorter sessions.

Listening material

The Student's Book cassette contains:
   Listening Presentation material
   Listening Models for student interaction
   Extended Listening Comprehension material
   Recorded Examples of Practice material

1.3   The syllabus

Meanings into Words covers seven broad functional areas of language:
1 *Action*
   This area consists of language used for talking about the desirability and possibility of action: initiating action in oneself and other people, and commenting on one's own actions and the actions of other people.
2 *Description*
   This area consists of language used for 'physical' description of places, things and people: their appearance, their features, and their location.
3 *Personal information*
   This area consists of language used for giving information about yourself and other people: who you are, what you do, and what kind of person you are.
4 *Narration*
   This area consists of language used for talking about past events, and telling stories in the past. This includes information about when events took place, their sequence, their duration, and their circumstances.
5 *Past and present*
   This area consists of language used for relating the past and the present: present situations and their past origins, past events and their connection with the present, and actions and activities during the period 'up to now'.
6 *Comparison*
   This area consists of language used for comparing and evaluating: talking about similarities and differences, measuring differences, and assessing advantages and disadvantages.

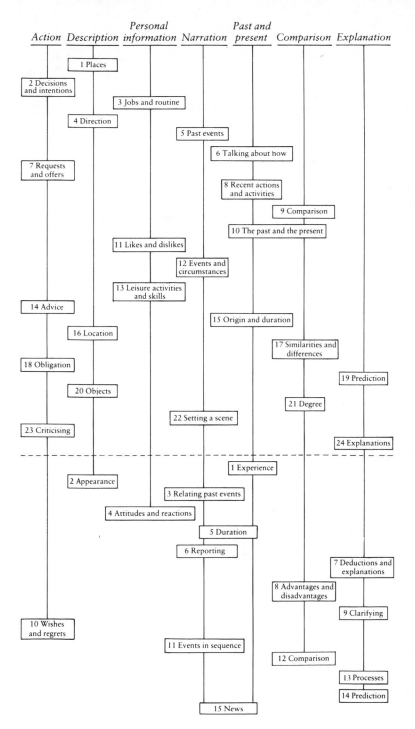

Table 1

7 *Explanation*
This area consists of language used for explaining things and speculating about things. This includes saying why and how things happen, establishing the truth about things, and drawing conclusions about the past, present and future.

Each of these seven areas is divided into a number of units, which are arranged in such a way as to provide (as far as possible):
– a natural and logical progression
– an increasing level of difficulty throughout the course
– maximum variety and motivation for the student.
Table 1 shows how each general area is divided into units, and how the units are arranged.
   For a detailed account of the linguistic background of the course, see **Part 2: Linguistic background**.

1.4 What the units contain

Each unit falls into two or three closely related sections. These sections deal with specific notions and functions of language, which are associated with particular structures and vocabulary. For example, Unit 10 (Wishes and regrets) falls into two sections; these are shown below, together with their related language:

	Functions/Notions	*Language*
Section 1:	Wishing for changes Imagining oneself differently	I wish / If only + would/could; I wish / If only + Past tense; If + Past tense...would...
Section 2:	Expressing regret Criticising oneself	I wish / If only + Past Perfect tense; If + Past Perfect tense; should(n't) have done; could/needn't have done.

The overall organisation of the unit is very simple: each language area is dealt with in turn, and the unit ends with a Free Practice activity and an extended Listening or Reading Comprehension. New language is taught in the following stages:
– Presentation (including some basic manipulation practice)
– Practice
– Free Practice
This presentation–practice sequence is repeated several times in the unit, and may occur more than once within a single section, depending on the language being taught. The final Free Practice activity usually draws on language from all sections of the unit.
   Table 2 shows the organisation and contents of three typical units.

Unit 1
Experience

1.1 EXPERIENCES AND ACHIEVEMENTS
Presentation of: Present Perfect and Past Simple.

1.2 LISTING EXPERIENCES AND ACHIEVEMENTS
Practice
Writing

1.3 HAVE YOU EVER...?
Presentation of: Present Perfect Passive forms.
Practice

1.4 LEISURE ACTIVITIES
Practice
Free practice

1.5 FAMILIAR AND UNFAMILIAR EXPERIENCES
Presentation of: be used to + active and passive gerund forms.
Practice

1.6 NEW EXPERIENCES
Practice

1.7 JOBS
Free practice

1.8 APPLYING FOR A JOB
Reading
Writing

Unit 8
Advantages and disadvantages

8.1 GOOD AND BAD EFFECTS
Presentation of: 'Effect' verbs.
Practice

8.2 PROS AND CONS
Practice

8.3 ADVANTAGES AND DISADVANTAGES
Presentation of: (dis)advantage of / drawback of / good (bad) thing about / trouble with.
Free practice
Writing

8.4 COURSES OF ACTION
Presentation and practice of: ought to, ought not to, there's no point in, might as well.

8.5 ADVISING ON A CHOICE
Practice

8.6 DON'T DO IT: READING GAME
Practice

8.7 WHAT WOULD HAPPEN?
Presentation and practice of: If + Present tense... will..., If + Past tense... would...
Free practice
Writing

8.8 DISHWASHERS
Reading
Writing

Unit 10
Wishes and regrets

10.1 I WISH & IF ONLY
Presentation of: I wish / If only + would/could and Past tense.
Practice

10.2 CONFLICTING WISHES
Practice of: I wish / If only + Past tense; If + Past tense.

10.3 FANTASIES
Free practice
Writing

10.4 REGRET
Presentation and practice of: I wish / If only + Past Perfect tense; should(n't) have done; If + Past Perfect tense.

10.5 FEELING SORRY FOR YOURSELF
Practice

10.6 I WISH I'D KNOWN: READING GAME
Practice of: could/needn't have done.

10.7 WISHES AND REGRETS
Free practice
Writing

10.8 CHILDREN'S WISHES
Reading

Table 2

5

1.5   Stages in a unit

Here is a brief description of the stages of the presentation–practice sequence, as well as writing, listening comprehension and reading comprehension.

Presentation

Presentation techniques in the course are designed to suit the requirements of the language being taught, and to involve students as much as possible. There is therefore a wide variety of presentation material: language may be presented by reading, by listening, or by written examples, and the presentation often involves interpretation and class discussion.

The Presentation stage may include some basic manipulation practice of new structures.

Practice

This stage is concerned with controlled practice of new language. It ranges from simple manipulation of structures to more imaginative practice in which students use language in realistic situations.

Practice is usually done in pairs or small groups, and is concerned with appropriate use of language as well as with accuracy.

Free practice

At this stage students are not limited to using particular language. Practice may take the form of role-play, group discussion, or students talking about themselves, and gives them a chance to practise the language they have learnt in a wider context.

Writing

Practice in writing is provided at any stage of the unit where it is appropriate. It usually takes the form of paragraph writing, either based on classroom discussion or as a follow-up to listening or reading comprehension.

Listening/Reading

Each unit ends with a reading or a listening passage which features (but goes beyond) the language of the unit. These passages are followed by comprehension questions, but may also be used as a basis for note-taking, writing, discussion or role-play.

1.6   How the units work

Here is a more detailed picture of a typical unit, showing what happens in the classroom at each stage:

Unit 8   Advantages and disadvantages

8.1 – 8.3 Language functions:	describing good and bad effects evaluating advantages and disadvantages

8.1 GOOD AND BAD EFFECTS

Presentation
'Effect' verbs with infinitives and gerunds

Students listen to a story about an imaginary island. They reconstruct sentences from the story, focussing on 'effect' verbs (e.g. enable, prevent). Teacher presents 'effect' verbs.

Practice

In pairs, students improvise an interview based on the story they heard.

8.2 PROS AND CONS

Practice
'Effect' verbs

In groups, students have short conversations about a range of topics, based on an example.

8.3 ADVANTAGES AND DISADVANTAGES

Presentation
(dis)advantage of / drawback of / good (bad) thing about/trouble with.

Students read a short passage about the advantages and disadvantages of being unemployed. Teacher presents 'advantage/disadvantage' structures. Students use the structures to discuss the passage.

Free practice

In groups, students discuss the advantages and disadvantages of living abroad.

Writing

Students write a paragraph based on their discussion.

8.4 – 8.6 Language functions:	advising on a course of action making suggestions

8.4 COURSES OF ACTION

Presentation and practice
ought (not) to
there's no point in + -ing
might as well

Students look at two pictures with captions in which people are deciding on a course of action. Teacher presents 'ought (not) to' 'there's no point in' and 'might as well'. Students change sentences, using these structures.

8.5 ADVISING ON A CHOICE

Practice
there's no point in + -ing
it's not worth + -ing
might as well

In groups of three, students have short conversations, based on an example.

8.6 DON'T DO IT: READING GAME

Practice
you'd better not
there's no point in + -ing
it's no use + -ing

In groups, students read sentences and match them together, changing them to include the new structures.

8.7 Language functions: evaluating advantages and disadvantages of a course of action imagining possible consequences

8.7 WHAT WOULD HAPPEN?

Presentation and practice
If + Present tense ... will...
If + Past tense ... would...

Students read a short passage about someone who is about to leave school. They discuss what he might do and what the consequences might be. Teacher presents the two types of conditional structure.

Free practice
This activity uses language from the whole unit.

In groups, students tell each other about a difficult choice they have to make, and ask the others' advice.

Writing

Students write a letter giving advice, based on their discussion.

8.8 DISHWASHERS

Reading

Students read an extended passage about the advantages of dishwashers. In groups, they answer comprehension questions.

Writing

They make notes from the passage and write a summary.

1.7 The Activities pages

The Activities pages occur after every unit. These recycle and combine language learnt in previous units, and provide an opportunity for extended free speaking and writing.

Activities pages contain either two or three activities:

1 A free oral activity. This may take the form of a role-play, a discussion or a game.
2 A free writing activity. Students are given a choice of composition titles, which may be related to the oral activity.
3 Situations (every three units only). These draw on interactional language from the units. They are an oral equivalent of the written Progress tests.

1.8   Other components

The other components of the course are the Workbook, the Drills and the Test Book. These are all supplementary material, and are intended to be used throughout the course at the teacher's discretion.

The table below shows how material from the Student's Book, the Workbook, the Drills cassette and the Test Book fit together over a three-unit cycle:

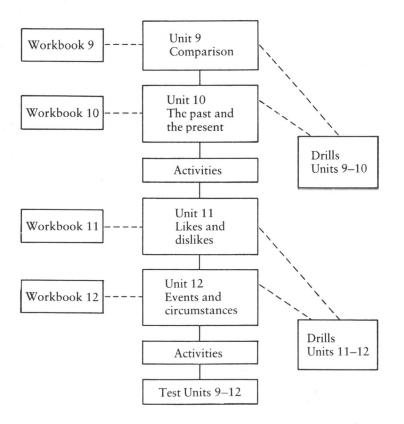

1.9   The recorded material

The *Upper-Intermediate Course* is accompanied by two cassettes. These are:
Student's Book cassette
Drills cassette

Student's Book cassette

This cassette contains four kinds of material:

1 *Listening Presentations*, which are used to present new language. Transcripts are given in the appropriate place in Part 4, and in the back of the Student's Book for reference.

2 *Short Listening Models*, which show students the kind of language they are expected to use. Transcripts are given in the appropriate place in Part 4, and in the back of the Student's Book, for reference.
3 *Listening Comprehension Passages*, which are used for comprehension and as a basis for writing and discussion activities. Transcripts are given in the appropriate place in Part 4, but not in the Student's Book, as it is important that students do not read them before doing the comprehension exercise. Transcripts can be typed and duplicated for students if teachers want them to be able to read the passages afterwards.
4 *Recorded Examples of practice exercises*, which can be played to the class before doing an exercise, and which give a guide to intonation. These follow examples printed in the Student's Book.

Material on the tape follows a 'chronological' order, i.e. the order in which it would be used.

A full contents list of the cassette is given in Appendix A.

Drills cassette

This cassette contains 29 drills, divided into five Sessions. The transcripts of the drills are in Appendix B, and the *examples* given for each drill are shown on the Drills pages at the back of the Student's Book.

1.10   Vocabulary

Vocabulary is systematically taught when:
1 it is linked with important grammar (e.g. 'attitude' verbs and adjectives, reporting verbs).
2 it is linked with a major topic area (e.g. names of facial features, 'character' adjectives).

Such vocabulary is specifically practised both in the units and in Workbook exercises.

Other incidental vocabulary in exercises and reading and listening passages is intended to be dealt with in its natural context as it arises.

The Progress Tests also contain a Vocabulary section which features important vocabulary from the previous three units.

1.11   Pronunciation and intonation

The course does not include any formal teaching of pronunciation or intonation. However, students are given plenty of exposure to spoken English in the form of listening comprehension passages, listening models, recorded examples and the drills. It is assumed that teachers can deal with any particular pronunciation and intonation problems as they arise.

1.12 Examinations

Together, the *Intermediate Course* and the *Upper-Intermediate Course* take students from an intermediate level to the level of the Cambridge First Certificate Examination, and can be used as a preparation for this and other examinations at this level. *Meanings into Words* develops all the language skills needed for FCE, and also gives practice in some of the examination skills. However, the course is not intended primarily to develop specific examination techniques, and students going on to take FCE are recommended to work with past FCE papers as a final preparation for the examination.

The table below shows how *Meanings into Words* would lead up to FCE (a) on a non-intensive five-hour-a-week course (b) on an intensive 15-hour-a-week course.

Five hours a week		*15 hours a week*
Term 1 Term 2 Term 3	*Meanings into Words* *Intermediate*	Term 1
Term 4 Term 5	*Meanings into Words* *Upper-Intermediate*	Term 2
Term 6	Final revision (past papers)	

Part 2: Linguistic background

Meanings into Words is a course in grammar and its use in communication. It sets out to teach the grammatical system of English in relation to the uses to which the learner will predictably want to put it. As the title indicates, we present the grammar of English as a means for putting into words many of the meanings that the learner will want to express in the process of using language for various communicative purposes.

We are concerned, therefore, with getting the student to develop an understanding and command of grammar in terms of *form, meaning* and *use*. This involves teaching the relations between form and meaning (the rules of the grammatical system itself) and also the relations between meaning and use (which Widdowson has called the 'rules of use'). In other words, it is important that the student learns to associate the choice of grammatical form or structure with the expression of a conceptual choice; we must also be sure that he can associate the making of conceptual choices with the performance of various types of communicative activity.

The general aims of the course are perhaps best seen as a concern to integrate traditional and communicative approaches to language teaching. We are convinced that there is an urgent need for materials which draw together and synthesise what is of value in 'structural' courses and in 'functional' courses, reconciling their different aims, supplementing them where they are deficient, and thus reducing the discrepancy between what they cover.

Materials derived from a structural syllabus have been justly criticised for failing to make explicit how their content relates to the student's communicative needs. Such courses seek primarily to ensure coverage of the major grammatical structures of English. They focus on teaching the accurate formation of the structures themselves, and on teaching how contrasts in grammatical form serve to express contrasts of meaning – conceptual distinctions. However, they tend to leave the student to work out for himself when he will have a *use* for the expression of these conceptual distinctions. Structural courses tend to teach form and meaning, but not use.

Many functional courses, on the other hand, have come under criticism for erring in the opposite direction. They start from categories of language use – communicative functions – and present the student with the language forms required for conveying them. However, they often fail to present those language forms as belonging to a coherent system of grammatical choices related to conceptual contrasts. There is nothing to explain how it comes about that particular forms realise certain functions – the student is simply presented with pairings of function and form which he can only commit to memory. This weakness results from an exaggerated preoccupation with 'functions' at the expense of 'notions' – an overemphasis on language as an instrument of social interaction and a neglect of its equally important conceptualising function. For a conceptual as well as a functional element is present in every language act. Functional courses, then, teach form and use, but tend to leave out meaning.

We have tried to ensure that our approach avoids the shortcomings of both types of course by checking whether the relations between form, meaning and use are perceptible to the student at every stage. This has involved the following procedures:

1 In the case of grammatical areas normally only dealt with in terms of form and meaning we have introduced contexts of use. This is especially important where the grammar of English draws conceptual distinctions which are not made in the grammar of the student's own language. Information about use is important here not just for its own sake but also because it helps to clarify and reinforce the student's understanding of the meaning-distinction. We assume, for instance, that when the student sees the Present Perfect tense presented and practised for such purposes as stating one's previous experience, announcing news, describing changes, etc., he will more readily grasp its function as a verb form for referring to 'past events of current relevance'.

2 Even in the case of areas where form rather than meaning is the student's greatest difficulty (e.g. relative clauses) we have sought to ensure that structural practice takes place in contexts which illustrate use (e.g. differentiating between types of object).

3 In dealing with functions, we have tried to offer the student a better understanding of how they and their exponents are related through meaning by grouping them together in conceptually related sets. For instance obligation, permission, exemption and prohibition are systematically related to each other through the concepts of necessity and possibility, which are in turn typically expressed by certain modal auxiliary verbs.

4 Having once identified the major uses of key grammatical structures, we have subjected these uses of language to closer analysis to see what other grammatical material regularly occurs in the same type of context to express either the same meaning or a related meaning. For example, in considering the category 'describing people (function) by reference to their characteristic activities (concept)' as a typical use of the Present Simple tense, we found that in actual instances of this use speakers commonly add further conceptual information such as 'frequency/intensity' or 'proficiency'. This has led us to invite the student to go beyond simple statements like *She knits* and *He plays tennis* and to tackle sentence types like *She does a lot of knitting* and *He's not a bad tennis player*. Similarly, *be used to + -ing* is introduced into the same unit as the Present Perfect tense because both structures are used to state previous experience.

Part 3: How to use the course

3.1 Time considerations

Meanings into Words is a complete, self-contained course, which should be
worked through unit by unit. The *Upper-Intermediate Course* is designed to
last between 80 and 100 classroom hours, but the exact time it takes to
complete will depend on various factors, such as the level of the class and the
intensity of the course.

If the teacher finds that there is not sufficient time to cover all the material,
it is of course possible to leave out certain exercises without disrupting the
continuity of the course. We have not marked any particular exercises as
'optional' as we feel that this should be left to the individual teacher to decide:
the choice of which exercises can be left out will naturally depend on the needs
of the students (for example, the class as a whole may be very good at reading
or may have already fully mastered certain structures).

If, on the other hand, there is time to spare, the teacher may want to supple-
ment the course with extra listening, reading, writing or discussion material.

3.2 The Workbook, Drills and Test Book

The Workbook

The Workbook is designed to be used parallel to the units, and provides
homework material for the students, covering the main points of each unit.

In the Teaching Notes, there are cross-references indicating appropriate
times to set individual Workbook exercises.

Workbooks can be taken in for correction, or answers may be gone through
in class.

The Drills

The Drills can be used in two ways:
1 with the whole class in language laboratory lessons
2 by individual students as self-access material.
Each Lab Session covers important structures from three units, and should be
used towards the end of the second unit, or afterwards for revision.

On the tape, each drill begins with at least two examples, and these examples
are given in the Drills pages at the back of the Student's Book, so that students
can refer to them while they are doing the Drills.

The Test Book

The Progress Tests are designed to check students' progress every three units, and can be used in two ways:
1 as formal classroom tests, which are taken away and marked
2 as informal 'round the class' tests, or as revision material.
The Test Books are intended to be reusable, and kept by the teacher in class sets, and there is no space provided for students to write their answers. When using the book for formal tests, students should write their answers on pieces of paper, or answer sheets can be typed and duplicated for them.

The Final Achievement Test covers both the *Intermediate* and the *Upper-Intermediate Course,* and can be used either as revision material or as part of an end-of-course examination.

The six photographs at the back of the Test Book can be used in oral tests. They will be found especially useful in preparing for Paper 5 of the Cambridge First Certificate Examination.

A guide to the answers can be found in Appendix C.

3.3   Elicitation

Elicitation plays an important part in presenting new language in the units. Instead of just 'presenting' the language to the students (e.g. by telling them or writing it on the board), the teacher elicits the relevant information from the students by asking questions. The presentation material may take the form of examples, a listening dialogue or reading passage, or even pictures, and the teacher uses this and his* own questions to establish the teaching point or to introduce new items of language.

An example of this is the presentation in 2.1, shown on page 16. The captions to the pictures illustrate the difference between *look, look like,* and *look as if/though,* without actually saying what that difference is. By asking questions (e.g. 'What's an ostrich?', 'What else do you think she *looks like?*', 'Give me another sentence with *looks as if...*'), the teacher establishes that *look* must be used with *like* before nouns and with *as if* or *as though* before whole clauses (or sentences). Once the students have got the main point, the teacher may then present the language formally before going on to the practice stage.

By eliciting, rather than giving a 'straight' presentation, the teacher is able to involve the students much more and focus their attention on the language being presented; he can also see more clearly what students know and do not know, and adapt his presentation accordingly.

---

* We refer to the teacher and student throughout this book as 'he' – this is not because we assume that all teachers and students are male but because the English pronoun system forces us to choose between 'he' and 'she'.

2.1 JUDGING FROM APPEARANCES

Presentation

How do we use: 1 look ...?
2 look like ...?
3 look as if/look as though ...?

3.4 Pairwork and groupwork

Many of the exercises at the Practice and Free Practice stages are designed to be done in pairs or small groups (four or five students). A typical pairwork or groupwork exercise has two or three stages:

1 A *preparation stage*, in which the teacher introduces the exercise and demonstrates the activity (e.g. by going through the examples, or doing the first one or two items with the whole class).
2 An *activity stage*, in which students do the exercise in pairs or groups. During this stage, all the pairs or groups work simultaneously and indepen-

dently, with the teacher going round the class listening, and giving help where necessary.

3 (optional) A brief *round-up stage*, where the teacher may ask individuals what answers they gave, or, after a discussion activity, what conclusions they came to.

The main advantages of conducting an activity in pairs or groups are:
– It gives more opportunity to students to practise language intensively and develop oral fluency.
– It provides a more 'natural' setting for students to use language – that is, face to face, and 'privately', rather than in front of the whole class.
– It encourages students to use English for real communication with one another.

Pairwork and groupwork can be used for a variety of activity types at different stages in a unit. At an early practice stage, they can be used for simple practice of structures in a situation or for a simple exchange of personal information. At freer practice stages, they can be used for role-playing, discussing topics of general interest, conducting interviews, and more extended exchanges of personal information.

3.5   Dealing with reading

Throughout the course there are reading texts (either Presentation Texts or Comprehension Passages) which the teacher reads with the class. There are various ways of doing this:
– The teacher reads the text while the students follow in their books.
– Students read the text silently.
– Individual students read the text aloud.
– (with longer texts) Students read the passage beforehand at home.

None of these is 'right' or 'wrong', and the choice should depend on what the teacher and students feel is best. In general, a varied approach is likely to be the most satisfactory.

   The main purpose of *Presentation Texts* is to show how particular language is used in context or to provide a stimulus for language practice. Because of this, comprehension of the passage is only a preliminary stage, and is dealt with quite quickly.

   In *Reading Comprehension Passages*, on the other hand, comprehension of the passage is the main purpose of the activity, and any role-play, discussion or writing that may follow it can be regarded as an extension.

   The questions that follow a comprehension passage are varied in type, both to provide interest and to suit the needs of the passage. As well as straight factual questions, there are also 'implication' questions, and questions for discussion. For this reason, it is usually best to divide the class into small groups to answer the questions, and to go through the answers with the whole class afterwards.

3.6   Dealing with listening

There are four kinds of listening material in the units. These are:
Listening Presentations
Listening Models
Listening Comprehension Passages
Recorded Examples

Listening presentations

The main purpose of *Listening Presentations* is to focus students' attention on new language items. Because of this, as with Reading Presentations, general comprehension is only a preliminary stage. In general, the procedure is as follows:
1 The teacher plays the tape once, and asks general comprehension questions.
2 The teacher plays the tape again, pausing where necessary, and asks questions about specific language points. It may be necessary to play the tape more than once at this stage.

Listening Models

Listening Models are dealt with in a similar way to Listening Presentations, but their function is rather different: they occur at the Practice stage, and act as loose models of the kind of language that students are expected to use in an activity. The activity might take the form of a discussion, an exchange of personal information or a role-play. In general, the procedure is as follows:
1 The teacher plays the tape once, and deals quickly with any new language items.
2 The teacher plays it a second time.
3 The teacher divides the class into pairs or groups for the activity.

Listening Comprehension Passages

As with Reading Comprehension Passages, *Listening Comprehension Passages* are intended to develop comprehension skills. The way Listening Comprehension passages are dealt with depends on whether they are used in the classroom with the teacher playing the tape recorder, or in the language laboratory.

In the classroom
1 *either* The teacher plays the whole passage once and asks a few general comprehension questions.
   or The teacher stops the tape periodically, and asks general questions as he goes along.
2 The teacher plays the passage again. This time he stops frequently and repeats sections of the passage (and even phrases) where necessary, and deals with each question in turn.
3 When all the questions have been dealt with, the teacher plays the tape once more straight through, as a round-up. At this point, duplicated copies of the passage can be given out to the students.

In the language laboratory

In many ways, the language laboratory is the ideal place to conduct a listening comprehension: students can work individually at their own speed, and the teacher is free to give help to individual students as they need it. The procedure is as follows:

1 The passage is recorded onto students' machines, and the machines are then put on student control.
2 Students work through the questions at their own speed. They listen to the tape, pause, and repeat sections as they need to.
3 When most students are coming towards the end, the teacher stops the machines, and discusses the answers with the class.

Recorded Examples

The *Recorded Examples* are an 'optional extra', and may be played once through to introduce an exercise at the Practice stage, while students follow in their books. They are particularly useful where intonation plays an important part in an exercise.

Part 4: Teaching notes

The teaching notes for each unit begin with a summary of what the unit contains, comprising:
– a brief description of the main language taught in the unit;
– a diagram which shows how the unit is organised;
– an *Assumed knowledge* section which shows what language the student should have already covered at an earlier stage. In this section, cross-references to Intermediate units are provided for the benefit of those who wish to refer back to the Intermediate Course.
    Notes for each exercise contain:

1 A description of the *language* introduced in the exercise (intended mainly for the teacher's own information) e.g. in 1.3:

> **Language:** Present Perfect tense for asking and talking in general about experiences.
> Past tense for giving details of an experience.
>
> *Note*: This exercise practises questions and answers using active and passive forms and the structure *have something done* (the 'have' passive).

2 Notes on suggested *procedure* for conducting the exercise (including ideas for presentation and practice). Numbers in brackets refer to questions in the Student's Book.
    Language in boxes is intended as presentation material that the teacher can write on the board, or build up by eliciting information from the students e.g. in 1.3:

> We <u>ate</u> Japanese food last weekend.
> – <u>Have</u> you ever <u>eaten</u> Japanese food?
>
> Someone <u>shouted</u> at me in the street this afternoon.
> – <u>Have</u> you ever <u>been</u> <u>shouted</u> at?
>
> Someone <u>stole</u> my bike last night.
> – <u>Have</u> you ever <u>had</u> your bike <u>stolen</u>?

Answers to some exercises are given. Numbers in brackets refer to questions in the Student's Book.

Cross-references to the Workbook

At the end of the notes to individual exercises there may be a cross-reference which indicates an appropriate point to set Workbook homework exercises, e.g. ▶ **W2 Ex 3** ◀ refers to Workbook Unit 2, Exercise 3.

Listening symbols

The symbol ▭ indicates that the exercise is accompanied by an essential piece of listening (Listening Presentation, Listening Model or Listening Comprehension). The text of the recorded material is included in the notes for that exercise.

The symbol ▭ indicates that the written example in the Student's Book is also recorded on the tape, and can be played to the class before they do the exercise. The texts of the Recorded Examples are not included in the teaching notes.

Unit 1 Experience

This is one of a series of units concerned with relating *the past and the present*. It deals with language for talking about experiences and achievements, giving details of experiences, and talking about familiar and unfamiliar experiences.

The unit falls into two sections, followed by a general Free Practice exercise and a Reading Comprehension. The first section is concerned with talking in general and in detail about experiences and achievements; it contrasts the Present Perfect and Past Simple tenses and practises more advanced structures using the Present Perfect, including passive forms. The second section is concerned with talking about how familiar or unfamiliar experiences are; it practises structures with *be used to* and active and passive gerunds, and shows the relationship between *be used to* and the Present Perfect tense.

Assumed knowledge

Before beginning this unit, students should be familiar with:
Use of the Past Simple and Continuous for narration (Intermediate Units 5, 12, 22).
Use of the Present Perfect Simple for talking about recent events and actions (Intermediate Units 8, 10, 15).
Active and passive gerunds (Intermediate Unit 11).
The structure *have something done* (Intermediate Units 1, 11).

1.1 EXPERIENCES AND ACHIEVEMENTS
Presentation of: Present Perfect and Past Simple.

1.2 LISTING EXPERIENCES AND ACHIEVEMENTS
Practice
Writing

1.3 HAVE YOU EVER...?
Presentation of: Present Perfect Passive forms.
Practice

1.4 LEISURE ACTIVITIES
Practice
Free practice

1.5 FAMILIAR AND UNFAMILIAR EXPERIENCES
Presentation of: be used to + active and passive gerund forms.
Practice

1.6 NEW EXPERIENCES
Practice

1.7 JOBS
Free practice

1.8 APPLYING FOR A JOB
Reading
Writing

1.1 EXPERIENCES AND ACHIEVEMENTS   Presentation

> **Language:** Use of the Present Perfect and Past Simple
> tenses for talking about experiences and
> achievements *up to now.*
>
> *Note*: The aim of the exercise is to give general insight and
> to check that students understand how these tenses are
> used.

1 Read the passages. After each one, ask students to tell you where they might see the passage and what it's about.
   Possible answers: (A) Part of a letter of application for a job in publishing (perhaps as a travelling representative); outlining the applicant's qualifications and experience.
   (B) Part of a 'blurb' on the back or inside the front cover of a novel; giving a brief description of the author's life and work.
   (C) Part of a letter (a reply) written by someone who's about to live on his own in a cold, remote place (perhaps in the Arctic or Antarctic).
   (D) Part of a biography or newspaper article; describing an earlier period in Martin Kingsley's life.

2 Discuss the questions, eliciting as much information as you can. Establish that in the first three paragraphs:
   (1) The Present Perfect tense is used for saying what experiences the people have had up to now, without reference to specific times or the order in which they happened:
   e.g. I have visited most of the major European capitals (= at various times).
   I have never been directly involved in publishing (= at any time).
   I've lived on my own before (= at some time).
   (2) The Past tense is used for describing experiences with reference to a specific time or period in the past:
   e.g. I studied French *at university.*
   His fourth novel won the Pulitzer Prize *in 1969.*
   In Greenland the temperature was often minus 40°.
   (3) Whereas the first three paragraphs describe experiences *up to now,* Paragraph D describes Martin Kingsley's experiences *during a period in the past* (i.e. up to the time he became successful), so only the Past tense is used.

1.2 LISTING EXPERIENCES AND ACHIEVEMENTS

> **Language:** Use of the Present Perfect and Past Simple for
> listing experiences and achievements *up to
> now.*

Practice

1 Read Paragraph B in the preceding exercise again.
2 Ask students to suggest sentences for (1) round the class:
   e.g. She's won 15 Oscars.
           She appeared with Richard Burton in the film *Las Vegas*.
3 Divide the class into groups to make up sentences for (2)–(5).

Writing

The paragraphs can be written individually or in groups, or done for homework.
► W1 Ex 1 ◄

1.3 HAVE YOU EVER...?

> **Language:** Present Perfect tense for asking and talking in general about experiences.
> Past tense for giving details of an experience.
>
> *Note*: This exercise practises questions and answers using active and passive forms and the structure *have something done* (the 'have' passive).

Presentation 🔲

This exercise begins with a Listening Model. (See 'Dealing with listening' in Part 3.)

A: Do you know at the weekend, we went out and had a meal in a Japanese restaurant. And it was absolutely amazing, I mean they gave us all this raw fish and stuff, and it was terribly neat and tidy, beautifully presented and quite different from anything I'd expected. Have you ever eaten Japanese food?

B: Yes, I have but only once. A friend took me to a Japanese restaurant to celebrate his birthday and we had sukiyaki or something – I don't know. I didn't like it at all to be honest.

A: Do you know, someone shouted at me in the street this afternoon. I was walking along you know, just minding my own business when this man came up and started shouting at me, started calling me names. I couldn't believe it. Have you ever been shouted at in the street like that?

B: No, I haven't, not like that. Er, well I have been shouted at but it was by a policeman. I mean it was a bit different. You see, I was driving and I drove straight through a red light.

A: Oh dear, someone stole my bike last night. I'm furious because it was entirely my own fault. I went to a party and I just left it outside the house where the party was without a padlock on. Not surprisingly when I came out it was gone. Have you ever had your bike stolen?

B: Yes, I have. Mine was stolen about a month ago as a matter of fact. I did exactly the same thing as you – I left it in the street without the padlock on. Luckily I got it back.

Play the tape. Students answer the questions. From their answers, build up this table on the board, showing the different forms:

> We <u>ate</u> Japanese food last weekend.
> – <u>Have</u> you ever <u>eaten</u> Japanese food?
>
> Someone <u>shouted</u> at me in the street this afternoon.
> – <u>Have</u> you ever <u>been</u> <u>shouted</u> at?
>
> Someone <u>stole</u> my bike last night.
> – <u>Have</u> you ever <u>had</u> your bike <u>stolen?</u>

Practice

1 Look at the five remarks, and establish what questions the person would ask.
   e.g. (1) Have you ever been fined for a parking offence?
   (2) Have you ever had your picture printed in the newspaper?
2 Divide the class into groups to do the exercise. Each time, students should give details of the most similar experience they have had to the ones in the list.
   ▶ W1 Ex 2 ◀

1.4 LEISURE ACTIVITIES

> **Language:** Present Perfect tense questions for asking about experiences.
> Structures with superlative adjectives for talking about outstanding experiences.
>
> *Note*: This exercise revises structures and vocabulary for talking about leisure activities (see Intermediate Unit 13).

Practice

1 Ask students to make questions from the prompts. Point out the use of structures with superlative adjectives, and write these examples on the board:

What is the	highest most dangerous	mountain you'<u>ve</u> ever climb<u>ed</u>?

| The | highest
most dangerous | mountain I've ever climbed is/was
the Matterhorn. |

Possible questions: Have you climbed a lot (of mountains)? Have you done a lot of
   climbing/mountaineering?
   How many mountains have you climbed?
   Have you been to the Alps / climbed in the Alps?
   What's the highest mountain you've ever climbed?
   What's the longest time you've ever spent on a mountain?
   What's the most dangerous situation you've ever been in?
   Have you ever had to be rescued? Have you ever rescued anyone?

   Have you done a lot of sailing?
   Have you ever sailed on the open sea?
   Have you ever sailed single-handed?
   What's the furthest you've ever sailed in a yacht?
   What's the longest time you've spent on a yacht?
   What's the biggest yacht you've ever sailed in?
   Have you ever capsized?

2 Divide the class into pairs to interview each other. One student in each pair
   can be the mountain-climber, the other the yachtsman.

Free practice

1 Staying in their pairs, students take it in turns to interview each other. They
   should, of course, talk only about experiences they have had in connection
   with their leisure activities.
2 As a round-up, ask individual students to tell you what their partner's
   leisure activity is and what experiences he has had.
   ▶ W1 Ex 3 ◀

1.5 FAMILIAR AND UNFAMILIAR EXPERIENCES

> **Language:** *Be used to* followed by:
>   i)   active gerund
>   ii) passive gerund
>   iii) gerund form of *have something done.*
>
> *Note*: Active and passive gerund forms were practised with
> 'like and dislike' verbs in Intermediate Unit 11.

Presentation

1 Read the text. Check general comprehension and prepare for the presentation
   by asking questions round the class:
   e.g. What brought about the change in Dawn and Rickie's life?
        What effect is their success having on their life-style?
        What effect is their success having on their singing?
        Do they think they can cope with the changes?

2 Write these sentences on the board:

They sing very informally.
They're invited to sing at social functions.
They often have things written about them.

Now ask the class what Dawn and Rickie *are used to*, and build up this table to show how the structures are formed:

They're used to	sing<u>ing</u> very informally.
	<u>being</u> invited to sing at social functions.
	<u>having</u> things <u>written</u> about them.

3 Point out that *to* in 'be used to' is a preposition, so it must be followed by a *noun* or *gerund*. Make sure students understand the difference between:
   He often sleeps on the floor.
   He's *used to* sleep*ing* on the floor.

   He *is* often laugh*ed* at.
   He's *used to being* laugh*ed* at.

   He often *has* his photograph *taken*.
   He's *used to having* his photograph *taken*.

4 Ask the class what other things Dawn and Rickie *are used to*, and what things they *aren't used to*.

Practice

1 Look at the first pair of pictures, and ask students to suggest how the girl's life has changed and what she is and is not used to:
   e.g. She's come from a small village, so she's used to meeting people she knows all the time. Now she doesn't know anyone, so she'll feel lonely, because she's not used to being alone.
2 Divide the class into groups to discuss the other pairs of pictures.
3 Ask each group to tell you some of the conclusions they came to.
▶ W1 Ex 4 ◀

1.6 NEW EXPERIENCES   Practice

Language:	Further practice of *not used to*.
	Present Perfect structures for talking about
	new experiences:
	I've never...before.
	This is / *It's*	*the first time I've ever...*

1 Look at the examples. Point out that:
   i) the three structures have roughly the same meaning
   ii) after 'It's/This is the first time...' the Present Perfect tense *must* be used.
      (We *cannot* say 'It's the first time I'm sleeping...'.)

2 Either do the exercise with the whole class, or let students think of continuations in groups, and go through the answers afterwards.
▶ W1 Ex 5 ◀

1.7 JOBS   Free practice

> **Language:** Free practice of language introduced in this
>   unit.

1 Look at the different jobs, and make sure students understand what they all
  are. If you like, briefly discuss with the class what qualifications and
  experience might be relevant to each job.
2 Divide the class into pairs. Give a few minutes for students to choose a job
  and to prepare for the interview.
3 Students take it in turns to interview each other.
4 As a round-up, ask individual students whether they found their partner
  suitable for the job or not, and why.

1.8 APPLYING FOR A JOB

Reading

For procedure, see 'Dealing with reading' in Part 3.

Answers: (1) (c)
        (2) (a)
        (3) Any three of: speaking English, travelling abroad, working as a tourist
            guide, dealing with problems.
        (4) (a) He's been to many countries in Europe.
            (b) He knows enough French and Italian to make himself understood
                and understand other people.
            (c) He's always got on well with the people on his tours.
        (5) (a) He would be able to talk knowledgeably about paintings, historic
                buildings, etc.
            (b) Rooms reserved but which turn out to be occupied, double rooms
                booked when single rooms were wanted, etc.
            (c) Complaints, injuries, people getting lost/robbed, problems at
                customs, etc.

Writing

The writing can be done in class or for homework. Encourage students to use
Anton's letter as a model but not, of course, to follow it too closely.

Activities (following Unit 1)

FLATMATE

> **Language:** This activity draws on language from Unit 1
> (Experience), and also Intermediate units
> concerned with Action, Description and Personal
> information. (See Table 1 on p.3.)

1 Choose four students to be 'flat hunters'. Divide the rest of the class into
   four groups, each group representing one of the four different sets of people
   already sharing a flat. The flat hunters prepare individually; those already
   living in flats prepare in their groups.
2 Each of the flat hunters 'visits' each flat in turn by going to each of the four
   groups and finding out about their flat.
3 When all the flat hunters have visited all the flats, ask each of them which
   flat they would choose and why. Also ask each group which flatmate they
   would choose.

COMPOSITION

> **Language:** The composition draws on language from Unit 1
> (Experience), and also Intermediate units
> concerned with Description, Personal
> information, and Comparison. (See Table 1 on
> p.3.)

The writing can be done in class or for homework.

Unit 2   Appearance

This continues the series of units in the Intermediate Course concerned with physical *description* of places, things and people. It deals with language for talking about the general appearance of people and things, and for giving precise physical descriptions of people.

The unit falls into two main sections, followed by a Listening Comprehension. The first section is concerned with describing what people and places look like, and with talking about general impressions of people. It practises structures with *look* and other 'sense' verbs, and the use of *seem* with infinitives. The second section is concerned with giving precise descriptions of people's physical appearance; it introduces a range of vocabulary for physical description and practises structures for talking about age.

Assumed knowledge

Before beginning this unit students should be familiar with:
Use of *has/has got* and *there is/are* for description (Intermediate Unit 1).
Present and past infinitives (Intermediate Unit 23).

2.1 JUDGING FROM APPEARANCES
Presentation of: look + adjective/like/as if.
Practice

2.2 LOOKS AS IF & LOOKS AS THOUGH
Practice

2.3 GENERAL IMPRESSIONS: SEEM
Presentation of: seem + infinitive.
Practice

2.4 CAUGHT BY THE CAMERA
Free practice

2.5 DESCRIBING PEOPLE
Presentation of: facial features; general physical characteristics.
Practice

2.6 GUESSING AGES
Presentation and practice of: approximate age.

2.7 POLICE DESCRIPTION
Free practice
Writing

2.8 A STONY HOME
Listening
Discussion

2.1 JUDGING FROM APPEARANCES

> **Language:** Structures with *look* for talking about the
> appearance of people and things:
> i)   *look* + adjective
> ii) *look like* + noun
> iii) *look* $\begin{vmatrix} as\ if \\ as\ though \end{vmatrix}$ + clause
>
> *Note:* Similar structures are used with the other 'sense'
> verbs: *sound, feel, smell, taste*. These are introduced in 2.2.

Presentation

Look at the pictures and captions, and play the tape. From the captions elicit how the verb *look* is used.
Establish that:
(1) before an adjective, *look* is used on its own:
    e.g. She looks terrific.
(2) before a noun, *look* must be used with *like*:
    e.g. It looks like a wedding cake.
(3) before a complete clause, *look* must be used with *as if* or *as though*:
    e.g. It looks as though it's shrunk.
Note: In American English, *look* + *like* can be used before a clause. In British English this is regarded as sub-standard.

Practice

The purpose of this section is to give basic manipulation practice of structures with *look*. Look at the three pictures with the class, and ask students to make sentences using the prompts:
e.g. He looks as if he needs a wash.
     He looks rather aggressive.

2.2 LOOKS AS IF & LOOKS AS THOUGH   Practice

> **Language:** Practice of *looks as if/though*.
> Other 'sense' verbs: *sound, feel, smell, taste*.

1 Look at the examples, and point out that *looks as if/though* can be followed by various tenses, referring to the past, present or future.
2 Either ask students to make sentences round the class, or let them talk about the situations in groups, and go through their answers afterwards.
   Note: The situations are deliberately ambiguous. You should encourage students to think of as many different comments as they can.

3 The second part of the exercise brings in other 'sense' verbs. Elicit these from the class as you go through the situations.
Note: These other 'sense' verbs can also be followed by an *adjective* or by *like + noun*. They are used in exactly the same way as *look*.
Possible answers: (6) They sound as if they're having a party.
           (7) It smells as if it's just caught fire.
           (8) It feels as though someone's spilt some lemonade on it.
           (9) It tastes as if someone's been using it for washing up.

▶ W2 Ex 1, Ex 2 ◀

2.3 GENERAL IMPRESSIONS: SEEM

> **Language:** *Seem* + present or past infinitive, for talking about one's general impression of someone or something.

Presentation

1 Look at the sentences and ask students to change them.

Answers: (1) He *seems* (to be) very friendly.
        He *doesn't seem* (to be) very rich.
        He *seems* (to be) happily married.
        He *seems* to be some kind of businessman.
        He *doesn't seem* to spend much time out of doors.
        He *seems* to watch television a lot.
        He *seems* to have lived a very interesting life.
      (2) (This is a discussion question.)

2 Establish that:
   i)   *Seems* is followed by *to + infinitive* (before adjectives 'to be' can be omitted).
   ii) For talking about the past, we use *seem + past infinitive* (*to + have + past participle*).
   iii) The negative of *seems to...* is *doesn't seem to...* This is commoner than 'seems not to...'.
3 Point out the difference between:
   e.g. 'He *looks like* a businessman' (=physical appearance) and 'He *seems to be* a businessman' (=general impression).

Practice

Ask students to make comments about Mr Harvey using *seem*. Point out that they should suggest *general conclusions* from the particular evidence given.
Possible answers: He seems to be afraid of dogs.
        He doesn't seem to be very keen on gardening.
        He seems to have lived in Africa at some time in his life.

He seems to know a lot of people in different places.
His children seem to be at boarding school.
He seems to have injured his leg.

▶ **W2 Ex 3** ◀

2.4 CAUGHT BY THE CAMERA Free practice

> **Language:** Free practice of language introduced so far in
> this unit.

1 Demonstrate the groupwork by looking at one picture with the whole class,
   and asking for as many comments as possible using *look* and *seem*.
2 Divide the class into groups to discuss the other pictures.
3 Ask each group to tell you what they said about one of the pictures.
   Possible answers: *Picture 1:* They look as if they've been poisoned.
   It looks like a demonstration.
   Picture 2: It looks like a man with a goat's head.
   The man seems to be sitting on something.
   Picture 3: He seems to have a beard made of bees.
   He looks as if he's got a very hairy chest.
   Picture 4: He looks as though he's about to knock his hat off.
   The other people look rather surprised.
   Picture 5: The man seems to be telling her something.
   She looks rather bored.

2.5 DESCRIBING PEOPLE

> **Language:** Expressions and vocabulary for describing
> people's physical appearance:
> i)   names of facial features
> ii) adjectives for describing facial features
> iii) language for describing general physical
>   characteristics.

Presentation 🔊

This is a Listening Presentation. (See 'Dealing with listening' in Part 3.)

The man has got straight, dark hair –
it's fairly short – he's got a parting,
...er... he's slightly bald – with a
receding hairline. He's got sideburns
on each side of his face. He's got a
square face, with quite a few wrinkles.
His nose is slightly crooked; he's got a
cleft chin.

The woman has shoulder-length wavy
blond hair. She's got quite a long face,
with a pointed chin, and her nose is
long and pointed, too. She's got thin
lips, and freckles, and she's got a
dimple in one cheek.

1 Play the tape. Students identify the two pictures.
  Answers: Pictures 1 and 5.
2 Play the tape again. This time students write the information in the table.
3 Look at the other pictures, and help students to complete the table, presenting new items as they occur. The table should include the following items, and any others you think are important:

Hair:	dark, black, blond, brown; straight, wavy, curly, fuzzy; long, short, shoulder-length.
Face:	square, round, oval, long, thin.
Eyes:	large, small, narrow, wide, slanting.
Eyebrows:	thin, thick, bushy.
Nose:	straight, pointed, snub, hooked, crooked.
Lips:	full, thin.
Chin:	pointed, cleft, double.
Special features:	beard, moustache, sideburns; fringe, parting, receding hairline; mole, dimple, wrinkles, freckles.

4 Ask students to suggest questions and answers for (4).
  Possible answers: (a) What (kind of) complexion has he got?
  (fair, dark, swarthy, etc.)
  (b) What height / how tall is he?
  (about 6ft tall, medium height, short, etc.)
  (c) What (kind of) build is he?
  (He's heavily/slightly built, slim, broad/narrow-shouldered, etc.)

Practice

1 [🔊] Play the example on the tape.
2 Demonstrate the pairwork by secretly thinking of a person in the class yourself and asking the class to guess who it is by asking you questions.
3 Divide the class into pairs to do the exercise. They take it in turns to think of a person.
  ▶ W2 Ex 4 ◀

2.6 GUESSING AGES   Presentation and practice

> **Language:** Contrast between:
> i) expressions for describing an approximate *date* (e.g. in the mid (middle) thirties)
> ii) expressions for describing approximate *age* (e.g. in his mid (middle) thirties)

1 Look at the examples. Build up these tables on the board to show the different structures:

i)	in the	early mid late	thirties

ii) in <u>his</u>	early mid late	thirties

Point out that i) means in the decade 1930–40, whereas ii) means between the ages of 30 and 40.

2 Do the first part of the exercise round the class:
   e.g. (1) Richard was born in the early thirties.
         So he is now in his early fifties.
3 Either do the second part of the exercise with the whole class or let them discuss the questions in groups and go through the answers afterwards.

2.7 POLICE DESCRIPTION

> **Language:** Free practice of language introduced in 2.5 and 2.6.

Free practice

1 Read the description with the class. Check general comprehension by asking questions:
   e.g. What's the man done?
       Where does he probably come from?
       What will he probably do if you approach him?
2 Divide the class into groups. Each group secretly chooses a person in the class, and together builds up a full description of him.

Writing

1 Working together, each group writes *one* description of the person they have chosen.
2 Ask one person from each group to read out their description. The rest of the class try to guess who the person is.
▶ W2 Ex 5 ◀

2.8 A STONY HOME

Listening 📼

This is a Listening Comprehension Passage. For procedure, see 'Dealing with listening' in Part 3.

Man: Now tell us about this picture, Lucy.
Lucy: Well it looks as though it's all made of stone. There are french windows going out through the wall, and you can see rocks at the other side. And in front of the french windows there's a table with

35

– a table made of stone with a stone tablecloth on it, and it's got a stone book, a stone bowl and...three apples? A stone bottle, most probably of wine, and a glass...(Made of?)...stone.

Man: Yes. Well, what do you think of this picture?

Lucy: It's interesting, because it looks as though maybe there was an earthquake – no, not quite an earthquake, a volcano, which lava spilt all over the things and made them stone.

Man: Ah, that's a great idea – I never thought of that.

Lucy: Even the floors, that have sort of wooden tiles, are made of stone.

Man: So you think it was a volcano that made – that turned this whole house, this whole living room into volcanic stone or ash, yes?

Lucy: Mm. But lava of the volcano.

Man: And if it wasn't that, what do you think it could possibly be?

Lucy: Maybe, well I don't think it would be quite probable but maybe the Stone Age came over it.

Man: Mm – everything went back and turned into stone you mean – sort of magic.

Lucy: Yes. Or maybe the Stone Age went on for such a long time it

buried this house and then it was uncovered again.

Man: Do you think it's a stupid picture?

Lucy: No.

Man: Why not?

Lucy: Because, erm...

Man: If you had to paint a picture like this, would you paint it in those colours and making everything look as if it was made of lava or rock?

Lucy: Well if I was painting the picture I'd make it more colourful. I'd paint the bottle a sort of greeny colour with a label on it, probably, the bowl of apples I'd paint a colourful bowl and red and green apples and the book I'd make a white cover and the glass I'd make..well the colour that it is, and the outside I'd paint trees and grass...(Blue sky?)...Yeah, blue sky.

Man: Mm. What sort of light has this picture got? Has it got sunlight?

Lucy: No it's got a sort of dark cavy light with a sort of gleam on it.

Man: To me it looks more like moon-light. (mm) Like, um, like a photo-graph, a negative photograph (Mm). Well tell us darling what would you call this picture? What name would you give it?

Lucy: A stony home, probably.

Man: A stony home? (Mm). Very good.

Answers: (1) It looks as though it's all made of stone.
It looks as though maybe there was an earthquake.
(2) Lava from a volcano turned the room into stone.
The Stone Age buried the house.
(3) (a) She'd make it more colourful and more realistic.
(b) (i) A greeny colour with a label on it.
(ii) With a white cover.
(iii) Trees, grass and blue sky.
(4) (a) A dark, cavy light with a sort of gleam on it.
(b) It looks like moonlight, or like a negative photograph.

Note: The adjective forms 'stony', 'greeny' and 'cavy' are typical of children's language. 'Stony' is usually used in other contexts (a stony field, a stony expression); 'greeny' = green, greenish; 'cavy' (like in a cave) is not normally used.

Discussion

Either conduct the discussion with the whole class, or let students discuss the questions in groups and ask them to tell you afterwards what conclusions they came to.

Activities (following Unit 2)

THE I.Q. GAME

> **Language:** This activity draws on language from Intermediate
> Unit 20 (Objects).

1 Read through the opening paragraph and discuss with the class:
   i) different kinds of intelligence tests
   ii) other things a brick could be used for.
2 Read out the sentences below, pausing after each sentence and asking for
   one guess from someone in the class.
   – It can be used for keeping a cupboard door shut.
   – You can use it for cleaning your fingernails.
   – You could use it for writing your name.
   – You can use it for testing whether a cake is done.
   – If you have a lot of them, you can make models with them.
   – They can be used for playing games.
   – You can use them for counting.
   – You can use them for filling holes.
   – If you have one, you can use it for getting food from between your teeth.
   – You can use it for lighting a fire.
   Answer: a match(stick).
3 Divide the class into groups. Either give each group an object or let them
   choose their own. (Suitable objects might be: pin, handkerchief, ruler,
   newspaper, tin can). Go from group to group, checking that they all understand what to do.
4 When each group has made their list and numbered it, students form new
   groups; each new group should contain at least one student from each
   original group. They take it in turns to read out their list of 'uses', stopping
   after each item to allow *one* guess from others in the group.

COMPOSITION

> **Language:** The compositions can be approached in various
> ways. Compositions (2) and (3) are likely to
> draw on the same language as the previous
> activity.

The writing can be done in class or for homework.

Unit 3   Relating past events

This is one of a series of units concerned with *narration* of past events; it incorporates 'narration' language introduced in the Intermediate Course. It deals with ways of talking about previous events, actions and activities.

The unit falls into two sections, followed by a general Free Practice exercise and a Listening Comprehension. The first section is concerned with relating past situations to previous events and activities, and practises the relationship between Past and Past Perfect tenses. The second section is concerned with giving additional 'background' information in telling a story, and practises non-defining relative clauses.

Assumed knowledge

Before beginning this unit, students should be familiar with:

Form and uses of Past tenses (Intermediate Units 5, 12, 22).

Form and uses of Present Perfect tenses (Intermediate Units 8, 10, 15, Upper-Intermediate Unit 1).

Form and basic uses of Past Perfect Simple (Intermediate Unit 22).

Relative clause structures (Intermediate Units 1, 20).

3.1 THE PAST PERFECT TENSE
Presentation of: Past Perfect tense.
Practice

3.2 PREVIOUS EVENTS
Practice

3.3 PREVIOUS ACTIVITIES AND ACTIONS
Presentation of: Past Perfect Continuous and Simple.
Practice
Writing

3.4 LOVE AT LAST
Free practice

3.5 ADDITIONAL INFORMATION: RELATIVE CLAUSES
Presentation of: non-defining relative clauses.

3.6 BACK-GROUND INFORMATION
Practice

3.7 IT HAPPENED TO ME
Free practice

3.8 A NIGHT TO REMEMBER
Listening

3.1 THE PAST PERFECT TENSE

> **Language:** Use of the Past Perfect tense in narration for going back to events that had taken place earlier.

Presentation

1 Read the passage, and discuss the questions, which are intended to focus attention on how the Past Perfect tense is used.

Answers: (1) The Tartan Army planted a bomb / Julia saw Paul Mason.
She was stopped at army checkpoints.
She joined the motorway.
She stopped for coffee.
(2) Julia joining the motorway and being late.
(3) Possible answers:
(a) ...she had been held up at army checkpoints.
(b) ...there had been snow on the Yorkshire coast.
(c) ...she hadn't expected to see Paul Mason.

2 Use the answers to the questions to establish that:

i) The Past Perfect tense is used for 'going back' from the past to earlier events. It is only used if the main story is already set *in the past*. If necessary, make this clear by writing these examples on the board:

> Mary <u>is</u> late — she <u>was</u> stopped by the police on her way to work.
> Mary <u>was</u> late — she <u>had been</u> stopped by the police on her way to work.

ii) Which events are told in the Past Perfect tense often depends on the point at which the narrator chooses to 'set' his story. In the passage, the story is 'set' at the point where Julia joined the motorway. Events that follow that are told in the Past tense; events that precede that are told in the Past Perfect tense.

Practice

1 Make sure students understand that each story is 'set' at the point where the arrow is – so all the events before that will be told in the Past Perfect tense.
2 Either let students discuss the paragraphs in groups, or let them write them, individually or in pairs.
3 Go through the answers.

Possible answers: (1) When Edward arrived at the station, Joan was already there. When she had come home from work, she had found Edward's note on the kitchen table. So she had quickly packed a suitcase and had taken a taxi to the station. Edward caught sight of her standing by the barrier. 'Good', he said, 'We're just in time'.
(2) Guy realised that the situation was hopeless. Most of Guy's friends had left when the war had broken out, but he had stayed. Then,

when the war had ended, he had expected everything to go back to normal. But it hadn't – the foreign companies had stayed away, business hadn't improved, and eventually his money had begun to run out. Reluctantly, he made a decision. He picked up the phone and dialled the American Embassy.

▶ **W3 Ex 5** ◀

3.2 PREVIOUS EVENTS   Practice

> **Language:** Past Simple and Past Perfect tenses for relating past situations to previous events.

1 [tape] Play the example on the tape. Point out that A's second remark is an explanation of something that had happened before.
2 Demonstrate the pairwork by asking students to suggest 'what had happened' in (1):
   e.g. He'd grown a beard and he'd started wearing glasses. His face had aged and his hair had gone grey.
3 Divide the class into pairs to do the exercise.
4 As a round-up, ask different students to tell you some of their 'explanations'.
▶ **W3 Ex 1, Ex 2** ◀

3.3 PREVIOUS ACTIVITIES AND ACTIONS

> **Language:** Past Perfect Continuous and Simple, for describing previous activities and actions.
>
> *Note*: As the text shows, this relationship is the same as that between the Present Perfect Continuous and Simple (see Intermediate Unit 8.4).

Presentation

1 Read the text, and ask students to 'transpose' it into the past. Establish that:
   i)   The text is *set in the present* ('I *feel* really exhausted (now)'), so these tenses are used:
        Present Simple and Continuous
        Present Perfect Simple and Continuous.
   ii) What the speaker says a few days later is *set in the past* ('I *felt* really exhausted on Friday') so these tenses can be used:
        Past Simple and Continuous
        Past Perfect Simple and Continuous.
   iii) The Past Perfect Continuous is used for previous *general activities*; the Past Perfect Simple is used for previous *individual actions*.

Practice

1 [tape] Play the example on the tape.
2 Demonstrate the exercise by doing (1) with the whole class.
   e.g. He'd been trying to find one for months.
      He'd done various temporary jobs.
3 Divide the class into groups to do the exercise.
4 As a round-up, ask different groups to tell you some of the things they
   suggested.

Writing

The writing can be done as a group writing exercise in class, with each group
writing about a different person, or it can be left for homework.
▶ W3 Ex 3 ◀

3.4 LOVE AT LAST   Free practice

> **Language:** Free practice of language introduced so far in
>   this unit.
>
> *Note*: The time at which the story is 'set' moves forward as
> the story develops, so that in each paragraph there are new
> opportunities for Past Perfect tense usage.

1 Look at the pictures with the class. Ask students to tell the story orally.
   Note: The pictures and sentences give the outline of the story only. Students
   should expand it with details of their own:
   e.g. Why had the holiday been a bore?
      What exactly happened when she went for a swim?
2 The writing can be done in class or for homework.

3.5 ADDITIONAL INFORMATION: Presentation
      RELATIVE CLAUSES

> **Language:** Non-defining relative clauses for giving
>   additional or 'background' information in a
>   narrative, used with Past and Past Perfect
>   tenses (Simple and Continuous).

1 If necessary, give your own presentation of relative clauses before doing the
   exercise. Use the following procedure: Write the sentence 'John shook me
   by the hand' on the board. Then give extra information about John (e.g. 'He
   was sitting in the corner', 'I hadn't met him before'). Ask students to
   incorporate each piece of information into the sentence as a relative clause.

From their answers, build up a table on the board showing different relative clause types:

People

John,	who was sitting in the corner,... who(m) I hadn't met before,... whose brother was in the army,... { who my sister was in love with,... { with whom my sister was in love,... }	(subject pronoun) (object pronoun) (possessive) (+ preposition)

Follow the same procedure to build up another table of relative clauses describing 'things', starting with the basic sentence 'The lorry burst into flames':

Things

The lorry,	which could do 50 m.p.h.,... which he had bought second-hand,... { which he had crossed Europe in,... { in which he had crossed Europe,... }	(subject pronoun) (object pronoun) (+ preposition)

2 Read the text, and point out how additional information could be added at the numbered points.
3 Ask students to incorporate each of the sentences into the passage, changing it into a relative clause.
4 Ask students to construct complete stories, choosing one relative clause for each space. This can be done round the class or in groups.

3.6 BACKGROUND INFORMATION Practice

> **Language:** Practice of language introduced in 3.5.

1 Either let students read the text and additional information individually, or divide the class into groups to discuss how the story fits together.
2 Ask students to tell the whole story.
3 As a possible extension, ask students to write the story, either in class or for homework.

The complete story: Mary, who had been in a deep sleep, was woken suddenly by a strange noise, which seemed to come from outside her window. She sat up, startled. Then she froze as she saw that the window, which she had locked securely the night before, was wide open. With a shock, she remembered that the servants, who she had laughed at only that afternoon for being superstitious, had all left, and that she was alone in the house. A floorboard creaked behind her. Turning, she saw an old woman, who was dressed entirely in black and whose mouth was twisted into a toothless grin. Suddenly, she realised who it was – it was her grandmother, who had died exactly a year before.

4 For the second part of the exercise, students should imagine possible additions to the sentences. Either ask for suggestions from the whole

class, or let students discuss the sentences in groups and go through the answers afterwards.

▶ **W3 Ex 4** ◀

3.7 IT HAPPENED TO ME   Free practice

> **Language:** Free practice of language introduced in this unit.

1 Demonstrate the activity by choosing one of the topics, and telling the class about an experience you had yourself. Bring Past Perfect tense forms and relative clauses into your story wherever they seem appropriate.
2 Divide the class into groups for the activity.
3 As a round-up, ask each group to choose their most interesting story, and tell it to the whole class.

3.8 A NIGHT TO REMEMBER   Listening 🔊

This is a Listening Comprehension Passage. For procedure, see 'Dealing with listening' in Part 3.

It was about half past eleven on a windy September night and Mr and Mrs Wilkinson had gone to bed early. They had put out the light and were just going to sleep when Mrs Wilkinson heard a strange noise coming from downstairs. Mr Wilkinson got up to investigate. When he reached the bottom of the stairs he noticed that the noise was coming from the dining room, and it sounded as if someone was trying to open the french window that led into the garden.

Mr Wilkinson was quite frightened, but he gathered up his courage, picked up a heavy walking stick and tiptoed into the dining room, moving round the side of the room so that he wouldn't be seen from the window. When he got to the window, he crouched down and peered cautiously round the edge of the curtain. To his relief, he saw that the noise was nothing more than a branch of a rose bush scraping against the window in the wind.

Meanwhile, however, the Wilkinsons' dog, who had been sleeping in the kitchen, had also woken up and had silently followed Mr Wilkinson into the dining room. While Mr Wilkinson was crouching by the window, the dog crept up behind him and affectionately rubbed his nose against his master's ankle. This gave Mr Wilkinson such a surprise that he gave a yell of terror, lost his balance and fell against the window, breaking the glass and cutting his hand quite deeply. He swore at the dog and kicked it out of the room.

Hearing all the commotion, Mrs Wilkinson now came rushing downstairs. When she saw what had happened, she took her husband back upstairs to the bathroom to treat his injured hand, which was bleeding profusely. Before she bandaged the wound, she cleaned it with pieces of cotton wool soaked in spirit, which she threw into the lavatory bowl when she had finished with them. Once this treatment was complete, Mr Wilkinson didn't feel like going back to bed, so he lit a cigarette to calm his nerves. Also, perhaps because of the excitement, he found that he needed to use the lavatory, and it was while he was sitting on the lavatory that he finished his cigarette and, without thinking, dropped the burning end into the bowl. The cotton wool that his wife had thrown into the bowl, being soaked in highly inflammable spirit, instantly burst into flames. Mr Wilkinson's bottom was severely burnt and he uttered another yell of terror.

This time, all Mrs Wilkinson could do was ring for an ambulance. It eventually arrived, and two men hurried upstairs with a stretcher, on which they laid Mr Wilkinson face down. They were a little puzzled when they saw that their patient had both a cut hand and a burnt bottom, so while they were carrying him down the stairs to the ambulance they asked him how these injuries had been caused. When Mr Wilkinson told them, they laughed so violently that they tipped him off the stretcher with the result that he fell down the stairs and broke his leg...

Answers: (1) (a) T (b) F (c) F (d) T (e) F (f) F (g) F
(2) He picked up a heavy walking stick.
He tiptoed into the dining room.
He moved round the side of the room.
(3) A cut hand (he fell against the window).
A burnt bottom (the cotton wool caught fire in the lavatory bowl).
A broken leg (he fell down the stairs).
(4) Have a cigarette; go to the lavatory.
(5) (a) They were puzzled. (b) They laughed.
(6) (See transcript.)

Activities (following Unit 3)

COMPUTERS: GOOD OR BAD?

> **Language:** This activity draws on language from Intermediate
> units concerned with Action and Explanation.
> (See Table 1 on p.3.)

1 Read the passage (which is part of a magazine article) with the
class, and check general comprehension by asking questions:
e.g. What might we use computers for in the future?
    What are some people afraid of?
If possible, let your questions lead to a general discussion of computers and
their advantages and disadvantages. Keep this relevant to your students'
interests by asking, for example, what *they* would use a computer for.
2 Divide the class into pairs. Students in each pair are either *both* A or *both* B.
Working together, they think what they will say.
3 Students form new pairs, so that each pair has one A and one B. They
improvise the conversation.
4 As a round-up, ask students what decision they came to.

COMPOSITION

> **Language:** The compositions are an extension of the
> previous activity, and draw on the same
> language areas.

The writing can be done in class or for homework.

SITUATIONS

> **Language:** The situations draw on language from Units 1, 2
> and 3.

Either: give a few minutes for students to read and think about the situations,
and then do them round the class.
Or: in pairs, students take it in turns to read and respond to the situations. Go
through them afterwards with the whole class.

Unit 4   Attitudes and reactions

This continues the series of units in the Intermediate Course concerned with giving *personal information* about yourself and other people. It deals with expressing attitudes to people and things, and describing reactions to experiences.

The unit falls into three main sections, followed by a Reading Comprehension. The first two sections are concerned with expressing attitudes; they practise a range of 'attitude' verbs and adjectives and some structures in which they are commonly used. These sections are followed by a writing exercise, in which the same language is used in the past to describe reactions to a particular event. The third section is concerned with describing people's characters, and introduces a range of adjectives.

Assumed knowledge

Before beginning this unit, students should be familiar with:
Verbs expressing likes and dislikes (Intermediate Unit 11).
Defining relative clauses (Intermediate Unit 20).

4.1 EXPRESSING ATTITUDES
Presentation of: verbs and adjectives for expressing attitudes.

4.2 VERBS AND ADJECTIVES
Practice

4.3 YOUR OWN ATTITUDES
Free practice
Writing

4.4 IF THERE'S ONE THING...
Presentation of: If there's one thing... it's ...
Practice

4.5 THE WAY
Presentation and practice of: attitude structures using 'the way'.
Free practice

4.6 REACTIONS
Writing

4.7 JUDGING CHARACTER
Practice of: 'character' vocabulary.

4.8 CHARACTER STUDY
Free practice

4.9 IT'S ALL RUBBISH REALLY
Reading
Discussion

4.1 EXPRESSING ATTITUDES   Presentation 🔊

> **Language:** Structures with verbs and adjectives for
> expressing attitudes:
> e.g. X *annoys* me.
>   I *am/get* annoyed by X.
>   I *find* X annoy*ing*.

This is a Listening Presentation. (See 'Dealing with listening' in Part 3.)

Presenter: Thank you. So that's the question. Angela, perhaps you'd like to start...

Angela: Well...er...on the whole I find television commercials extremely annoying. I mean, you're watching a film on television perhaps, and suddenly you're interrupted by these stupid commercials with a silly format which have nothing to do with the film you're watching, and they completely destroy your concentration. That really irritates me.

Presenter: Edward.

Edward: Well I must say I agree with Angela. I get particularly upset when I see these hordes of well-known people appearing in commercials, seemingly just to make a lot of money and pretending to believe in the product they're advertising. It upsets me. And that's what depresses me more than anything else, it's... ordinary members of the public actually believing what these commercials tell them. I think it's very sad.

Presenter: Sheila, do commercials have that sort of effect on you?

Sheila: Well, it's obvious that Edward's offended because he hasn't been asked to appear in a commercial. I couldn't disagree more actually. You see, it's true that not all commercials are good but a lot of them are very interesting and very amusing and some of them are even more interesting than the programmes. And of course there is a very important point about commercials whether you like them or whether you agree with them, whether you believe in them or not – is that the thing is, they do pay for the programmes. And without the commercials we wouldn't have the programmes at all, so I think that Angela and Edward are both being terribly one-sided and in fact their attitude really astonishes me.

Presenter: Well before we pass on to the next...

1 Play the tape. Students answer (1) and (2), which check general comprehension.

   Answers: (1) 'What attitude do the panel have to television commercials?'
   (2) (a) *Angela:* she finds them annoying; they interrupt the programmes; they're stupid.
   (b) *Edward:* they're used by famous people to make money; people are persuaded by them.
   (c) *Sheila:* they're often amusing and interesting; they provide money for the programmes.

2 Look at the example in (3) and check that students understand the meaning of the verb *annoy*. Play the tape again, pausing after each section, and get students to give you other 'attitude' words that are used; it may be necessary to elicit these by asking questions:
   e.g. Angela finds some commercials stupid – what effect do they have on her?

You should elicit these phrases:
> that irritates me; I get upset; that depresses me; he's offended; I find them
> amusing; I find them interesting; their attitude astonishes me.

3 Go back to the example in (3) and present the three possible forms by
writing these sentences on the board:

> I <u>find</u> television commercials <u>annoying</u>.
> Television commercials <u>annoy</u> me.
> I <u>am/get</u> <u>annoyed</u> <u>by</u> television commercials.

Point out that in the passive form, *be* and *get* are often alternatives. *Get* is
used especially to mean 'whenever it happens':
> e.g. I *am* annoyed by people who whistle (=in general).
>   I *get* annoyed by people who whistle (= whenever people whistle,
>   it annoys me).

Note: A few verbs, e.g. *impress, attract, fascinate, interest,* are not used
with *get*.

4 Ask students to change the sentences in (4) in the same way.

4.2 VERBS AND ADJECTIVES Practice

> **Language:** Adjective forms of 'attitude' verbs:
>   i) *-ing* ending (e.g. depress*ing*)
>   ii) *-ive* ending (e.g. offens*ive*).
>   Practice of structures introduced in 4.1.

1 Look at the example, and point out the two endings.
2 Working individually, students write the adjective forms.
3 Go through the answers, writing them on the board, and explaining the
meaning of any new words.

Answers:	-ING		-IVE
	exciting	shocking	impressive
	interesting	upsetting	offensive
	irritating	surprising	attractive
	confusing	astonishing	
		amusing	

Note: These are of course only a few of the many verb/adjective pairs that
follow this pattern. Others that occur in this unit are:
bore, amaze, fascinate, embarrass, terrify, disturb, disgust.

4 [🔊] Play the example on the tape. If necessary, demonstrate the groupwork
by doing (1) with the whole class.
5 Divide the class into groups of four to do the exercise. They should try to
practise all three forms, and use different words from the first part of the
exercise. If they like, they can of course disagree:
> e.g. Oh, really? I'm fascinated by politics.

▶ W4 Ex 1 ◀

4.3   YOUR OWN ATTITUDES

> **Language:** Free practice of language introduced so far in
> this unit.

Free practice

1 Look at the questions, and explain any new vocabulary.
2 Introduce the groupwork by telling the class about some of the things that embarrass you, using all three structural forms.
3 Divide the class into groups for the activity.
4 Let students continue in their groups for the discussion of beggars, door-to-door salesmen and nudists. This part of the exercise should draw on any of the vocabulary introduced in the unit so far.
5 As a round-up, ask each group what conclusions they came to about the three topics.

Writing

The writing can be done in class or for homework.
Note: This should be treated as a *free* paragraph writing exercise based on the discussion; warn students against 'over-using' the structures they have practised.

4.4   IF THERE'S ONE THING...

> **Language:** Expressing attitudes strongly, using:
> *If there's one thing* + Subject or Object
> Relative Clause.

Presentation

1 Look at the examples, and establish that:
   (a) contains a *subject* relative clause (with *that*); it is an emphatic way of saying 'People who jump queues get on my nerves'.
   (b) contains an *object* relative clause (without *that*); it is an emphatic way of saying 'I can't stand people who don't look where they're going'.
2 Working individually, students re-write the sentences.
3 Go through the answers.

Practice

1 [tape] Play the example on the tape. Demonstrate the exercise by doing (1) with the whole class. Point out that B should make a *generalisation* in his reply; so his answer in (1) could be '...people who make a mess' or '...people

49

who smoke during meals', '...people who don't use ashtrays', etc., but
not'...people who put cigarettes out on their dinner plate'.
2 Divide the class into pairs to do the exercise.
3 Go through the exercise, asking students what generalisations they made.
   Possible continuations: (2) ...who don't take care of other people's property.
                              (3) ...who don't pay attention when they're driving.
                              (4) ...who don't repay their debts.
                              (5) ...who don't look after their pets properly.
                              (6) ...who aren't punctual.
                              (7) ...who borrow things from their neighbours.

▶ W4 Ex 2 ◀

4.5 THE WAY

> **Language:** Use of *the way* as a sentence connective.
> Use of 'cleft sentence' structures, for isolating
> or emphasising information.
> Free practice of language introduced so far in
> this unit.

Presentation and practice 📼

This is a Listening Presentation. (See 'Dealing with listening' in Part 3.)

Presenter: ...we asked various people what they thought about the police...

A: Well, what I like about them is the way they're so helpful. You know – the way they can always find time to help when you need directions, if you're lost or something.

B: I resent the way the police react quite differently to different groups of people – I mean, for example, their reaction to young people and students, youths, they may have long hair, very short hair, skin heads – is quite different from people who are, you know, sort of middle-aged, they have well-spoken middle-class voices. It's quite wrong.

C: The thing that impresses me about them is the way they manage to keep control of crowds and things so effectively...I mean we've been to some wonderful functions here in London and it's tremendous...I mean they don't carry guns or anything like that. They're a great bunch of guys.

D: What I like most about them is the way they're so frightfully polite. I mean, I find that if ever I ask them a question, they call me 'Madam' and they're just generally polite. I do like them.

E: I get very annoyed by the way they ask you so many questions. They seem so slow and stupid sometimes which really gets on my nerves.

1 Play the tape. Students answer (1) and (2).
2 From these answers, establish how *the way* is used after 'attitude' verbs.
   Point out that it can be used in two ways:

i) meaning literally, the *manner* in which someone does something:
   e.g. I like the way he smiles.
ii) *not* meaning literally the *manner* but rather *the fact that* someone does something:
   e.g. I like the way he smiles all the time.
      (= He smiles all the time; I like that.)

3 Show how 'cleft sentence' structures are formed by writing these examples on the board:

Object type

I like the way he smiles all the time.	
What The thing that	I like about him is the way he smiles all the time.

Subject type

The way he smiles all the time impresses me.	
What The thing that	impresses me about him is the way he smiles all the time.

4 Students make sentences from the list, using any 'attitude' verbs they like:
   e.g. What I really hate about them is the way they never bother to learn local languages.
5 As an extension, ask students what else they like and dislike about tourists.

Free practice

1 Point out that in their discussion students can use any of the language introduced in this unit. If you like, demonstrate the activity by briefly commenting yourself on local TV programmes.
2 Divide the class into groups for the activity. Students take it in turns to be the reporter.
3 As a round-up, ask different 'reporters' to tell you what attitudes the people they interviewed had.
   ▶ W4 Ex 3 ◀

4.6 REACTIONS   Writing

> **Language:** Further practice of 'attitude' structures, used in the past to describe reactions to an experience.

1 Read the text. Ask students to suggest what kind of film is being described.
   Possible answer: Probably a romantic historical film about a child in the slums of London, perhaps based on a nineteenth-century novel (e.g. Dickens).

2 If you think it is necessary, do (1) orally, asking for sentences round the class.
3 The paragraphs can be written by students individually or in groups, or done for homework.
▶ W4 Ex 5 ◀

4.7 JUDGING CHARACTER   Practice

> **Language:** Vocabulary for describing a person's character.
>
> *Note*: Most of the items are adjectives, although a few nouns are possible (e.g. optimist, pessimist).

1 Look at the first pair of items with the whole class, and elicit the words *generous*, and *mean* and *stingy*.
2 Give time for students to look at the rest of the list, either individually or in groups, and think about possible answers.
3 Go through the exercise with the class, asking for suggestions and presenting new items as you go along. There are several possible answers each time – how many you introduce will depend on the level and interest of your class.
   Possible answers: generous; mean/stingy;
   bad-tempered / quick-tempered / irritable;even-tempered / calm / placid;
   kind / helpful / considerate; inconsiderate / selfish;
   light-hearted / cheerful / frivolous; serious / gloomy;
   optimistic / an optimist; pessimistic / a pessimist;
   credulous / gullible; sceptical / a sceptic;
   (over-)sensitive; insensitive / self-assured;
   friendly / sociable / outgoing / an extrovert; shy / reserved / an introvert;
   unreliable; reliable / conscientious;
   vain / conceited; modest.
4 The purpose of the second part of the exercise is to activate some of the vocabulary just introduced. Look at the example and elicit the most appropriate word.
   Answer: considerate.
5 Demonstrate the groupwork by thinking of a character adjective yourself, and telling a story to illustrate it. Students guess which word you have chosen.
6 Divide the class into groups for the activity.
▶ W4 Ex 4 ◀

4.8 CHARACTER STUDY   Free practice

> **Language:** Free practice of language introduced in this unit.

Either discuss the questions with the whole class, or let them discuss them in groups and ask them to report their conclusions afterwards.

4.9 IT'S ALL RUBBISH REALLY

Reading

For procedure, see 'Dealing with reading' in Part 3.

Answers: (1) (a) That the planets and stars can affect our character.
(b) Life on Earth is obviously affected by some outside forces (e.g. the Sun and the Moon).
(2) (a) They don't want to admit that they believe in them.
(b) He hid his Star Guide behind a newspaper; he smiled with embarrassment at the man sitting next to him.
(3) (a) It tells you briefly what will happen to you in the near future.
(b) It gives a picture of your character.
(4) (a) Likely to change from day to day.
(b) Having some skill at many things, but not really good at anything.
(c) Cannot feel deeply about anything.
(5) (a) 'Good': intellectual, quick-thinking, imaginative, generous, charming, interesting to talk to, wide variety of interests, successful. 'Bad': changeable, easily bored, indecisive, quick-tempered, can't concentrate, no depth of feeling, unreliable in love, dishonest.
(b) Many of the 'bad' items are consequences of the 'good' items (e.g. quick-thinking, therefore easily bored).
(6) (a) (i) It made him feel self-satisfied, and superior to those born under other signs.
(ii) Although he enjoyed reading about his good points, they didn't make him believe in astrology.
(b) It made him feel slightly worried, and more ready to believe in astrology.
(7) (a) Astrologers describe general characteristics that everyone recognises in himself.
(b) Relieved, because he no longer needed to believe in the Star Guide.

Discussion

1 Students discuss the questions in groups.
2 Ask each group to report their conclusions to the whole class.

Activities (following Unit 4)

FILM STILLS

> **Language:** This activity draws on language from Unit 3
> (Relating past events) and also Intermediate
> units concerned with Narration. (See Table 1
> on p.3.)

1 Divide the class into groups for the activity. Make sure that, in each group, all the students work together and that they all know their story.
2 Students form new groups, so that each group contains at least one person from each original group. In turn, they tell their story. Those listening should identify the pictures that appear in it.

COMPOSITION

> **Language:** This is an extension of the previous activity, and
> draws on the same language areas.

The composition can be written in class or for homework.

Unit 5   Duration

This forms part of two series of units – those concerned with *narration* of past events and those concerned with relating *the past and the present*. It deals with language for talking about duration in the past, in general, up to now and in the future.

The unit falls into three sections, followed by a Listening Comprehension. The first section is concerned with saying how long things lasted and how long it took to achieve things in the past; it practises past tense duration structures, including questions with *How long?*. The second section is concerned with saying in general how long it takes to do things, and practises structures with *takes* and *depends on*. The third section is concerned with talking about duration in different time periods, and practises duration structures using a range of tenses.

Assumed knowledge

Before beginning this unit, students should be familiar with:
Past tenses used in narration (Intermediate Units 12, 22, Upper-Intermediate Unit 3).
Present Perfect Simple and Continuous for talking about origin and duration (Intermediate Unit 15).
Structures for expressing intention and making predictions (Intermediate Units 2, 19).

5.1   HOW LONG?
Presentation of: past duration structures using 'How long?', 'for/until', 'in/by'.
Practice

5.2   YESTERDAY EVENING
Practice

5.3   LONGER THAN YOU EXPECTED
Presentation and practice of: not... before/till...; it was... before...
Practice
Writing

5.4   HOW LONG DOES IT TAKE?
Practice of structures with 'take' and 'depends on'.

5.5   WORK AND HOLIDAYS
Free practice

5.6   PAST, PRESENT AND FUTURE
Presentation of: duration structures using different tenses.
Practice

5.7   PERSONAL ENQUIRIES
Free practice

5.8   TOP DOGS
Listening
Writing

5.1 HOW LONG?

> **Language:** Structures for stating the duration of past
> activities and achievements:
> i) *How long...?* questions
> ii) Time prepositions: *for, until, in, by*.

Presentation

This is a Listening Presentation. (See 'Dealing with listening' in Part 3.)

Dialogue A
A: Hullo, Fred. Did you do anything exciting last night?
B: No, I just played cards with some friends.
A: You look pretty worn out. How long did you play for?
B: Oh, we played for about five hours. What about you?
A: Me? Oh I had to drive my sister to Heathrow. She was catching a plane to Canada.
B: How long did that take you?
A: It wasn't too bad. I got there and back by 11.30.

Dialogue B
A: Where were you last night?
B: I was baby-sitting for Wendy and Paul, actually.
A: Really? You must have been late, because I phoned you at midnight. How long did you have to baby-sit for?
B: Oh, I was there until about one in the morning.
A: That late? I hope they gave you a lift home.
B: Not a chance. I walked.
A: You're joking – it must be about five miles to your place from Wendy's. How long did it take you to walk all that way?
B: Not all that long, actually. I got home in less than an hour. I'm a fast walker.

1 Play the tape. Students listen, and then write the questions and answers from the two dialogues. Go through the answers.
2 Use Question (1) to establish that:
   i) *playing cards* and *baby-sitting* are *activities* (you spend a certain amount of time doing them, and then stop);
   ii) *driving to Heathrow* and *walking home* are *achievements* (the main idea of them is to complete a task, to get something finished).
3 Write this table on the board to show the different questions used:

ACTIVITIES	ACHIEVEMENTS
How long did you play cards <u>for</u>? How long did you <u>spend</u> playing cards?	How long did it take you to walk home?

4 Use Question (2) to establish that:
   i) *for* and *until* are both used in talking about *activities*:
   for refers to a period of time (e.g. for five hours)
   until refers to a point of time – the 'end-point' (e.g. until midnight)

ii) *in* and *by* are both used in talking about *achievements*:
   in refers to a period of time (e.g. in less than an hour)
   by refers to a point of time – the 'end-point' (e.g. by 2.00 a.m.)
Add these sentences to the table on the board to show the relationship
between the structures:

(ACTIVITY)		(ACHIEVEMENT)	
We played cards	<u>for</u> five hours. <u>until</u> midnight.	I got home	<u>in</u> less than an hour. <u>by</u> 2.00 a.m.

Practice

1 Go through the exercise with the class, asking students to give you questions
   and answers:
   e.g. (1) How long did they talk for?
             They talked for 20 minutes.
2 Look at the examples at the end of the exercise. Point out that they are
   alternatives to the structures already introduced. If you like, add these
   sentences to the table on the board:

(ACTIVITY)	(ACHIEVEMENT)
We <u>spent</u> five hours play<u>ing</u> cards.	<u>It took</u> me less than an hour <u>to</u> get home.

3 Ask students to go through the exercise again, using these structures.
   ▶ W5 Ex 2 ◀

5.2 YESTERDAY EVENING   Practice

> **Language:** Practice of language introduced in 5.1.

1 Play Dialogue A again as a model for the pairwork exercise.
2 If you think it is necessary, demonstrate the pairwork by doing (1) with the
   whole class.
3 Divide the class into pairs for the exercise.

5.3 LONGER THAN YOU EXPECTED

> **Language:** Structures for stating the length of time
>   between two events:
>   *X didn't happen for/till (+ time).*
>   *It was (+ time) before X happened.*

Presentation and practice

1 Look at the examples. Point out that:
   i) All the continuations refer to the length of time between two events.
   ii) The first continuation in each pair refers to a period of time (half an hour); the second continuation refers to the 'end-point' (twenty past).
2 Do the exercise round the class. More than one answer is possible in each case.

Possible continuations: (1) ...it was two weeks before the letter reached her.
   ...she didn't get the letter for two weeks.
   (2) ...I didn't get to bed till midnight.
   ...it was midnight before I got to sleep.
   (3) ...he didn't give it back for six weeks.
   ...it was six weeks before he gave it back to me.
   (4) ...it was three hours before it finished.
   ...it didn't finish for three hours.
   (5) ...it was Tuesday before I could hand it in.
   ...I didn't manage to give it to her till Tuesday.
   (6) ...he didn't turn up till after nine o'clock.
   ...it was after nine o'clock before he arrived.
   (7) ...they didn't finish it for nearly two months.
   ...it was nearly two months before they got it done.

Practice

1 Read the text, and point out that it tells us:
   i)   What the writer thought would happen.
   ii) Why it took longer than he expected.
   iii) What eventually happened and how long the delay was.
2 In groups, students construct 'oral paragraphs' that give similar information about the other topics.
3 Ask different groups what ideas they had.

Writing

The writing can be done in class or for homework.
► W5 Ex 3 ◄

5.4 HOW LONG DOES IT TAKE?   Practice 📼

> **Language:** Practice of:
>   i)   structures with *take* (see 5.1) used in the Present Simple to talk 'in general':
>   *How long does it take to...?*
>   *It* | *can take* | *... to ...*
> | *takes* |
>   ii) structures with *it depends on...*
>   iii) *If* + Present tense ('First Conditional')

This exercise begins with a Listening Model. (See 'Dealing with listening' in Part 3.)

A: How long does it take to drive
across London?
B: Well, that depends on the traffic. If
the roads aren't too busy, you can
do it in about an hour. But if you go
during the rush hour, then of course
it can take much longer.
C: Yes, of course it also depends on
how well you know the roads. If you
don't know the best routes, it can
take you hours to get through,
because you'll get stuck in one-way
systems and end up miles away from
where you want to go to. If I were
you I'd have a good look at a street
map before you set out...

1 Play the tape. Students answer the questions, which focus attention on structures with *depends*, *take*, and *if*.
2 Establish that *depends on* can be followed by:
   i) a noun:
       e.g. It depends on the traffic.
   ii) an indirect question:
       e.g. It depends (on) how much traffic there is.
   Note: Before a noun we must say 'depends *on*'. Before indirect questions, the *on* can be omitted.
3 Introduce the groupwork by looking at the first question with the whole class. Ask for suggestions for each topic:
   e.g. How long it takes to get to New York depends on how you travel, whether you fly or not, what kind of plane you fly in, where you start from, etc.
4 In groups of three, students discuss each topic as in the model. They take it in turns to ask the question.
   ▶ W5 Ex 4 ◀

5.5 WORK AND HOLIDAYS   Free practice

> **Language:** Free practice of language introduced so far in this unit.

1 Divide the class into pairs. Students in each pair are either *both* A or *both* B. Working together, they prepare their questions.
2 Students form new pairs, so that each pair has one A and one B. They take it in turns to interview each other.
3 As a possible round-up, ask individual students what they found out about their partners.

5.6 PAST, PRESENT AND FUTURE

> **Language:** Structures for expressing duration in different time periods:
> i)   in the *past*, using Past tense structures (introduced in 5.1)
> ii) in the period *up to now*, using Present Perfect Continuous tense (introduced in Intermediate Unit 15)
> iii) in the *future*, using Future tense and related structures (introduced in Intermediate Units 2 and 19).

Presentation

1 Read the text. Students answer Question (1), which focusses attention on the 'moment of speaking'.
Answer: early autumn, probably September.
2 Students answer Question (2). Use the answers to these questions to establish that:
(b) and (c) are activities that started and finished in the past, so the writer refers to them using Past tense duration structures:
Bob went to Arabic classes for a couple of months.
I spent most of the summer reading.
(a) and (e) are activities that started in the past and have been going on up to the present – so the writer refers to them using Present Perfect tense duration structures:
We've been preparing ... for a long time.
We've been packing since last Tuesday.
(d) and (f) are activities that haven't started yet, so the writer refers to them using Future tense duration structures:
We'll be staying ... for about a month.
We'll be away for about two months.

Practice

Either ask students to make sentences round the class, or let them look at the information in groups, and go through the answers afterwards.
Possible answers: Paul has been painting since 1970.
He spent three years studying at Art School.
He's been working in a studio in Amsterdam since 1976.
He's been working on a portrait of the Prime Minister for two months.
He'll be staying in Italy for three months.

Vanessa will spend two weeks training for the tournament.
She's been playing in tournaments since 1980.
She's been playing tennis since 1975, when she stayed in California for two months.

She played squash for two months last winter.
She'll be working as a tennis commentator for at least six months.
▶ **W5 Ex 1, Ex 5** ◀

5.7 PERSONAL ENQUIRIES   Free practice

> **Language:** Free practice of language introduced in this
> unit.

1 If you think it is necessary, prepare for the groupwork by asking students to suggest some of the questions they might ask each of the four people.
2 Divide the class into groups for the activity. Each student takes it in turn to be interviewed by the others in the group.
3 As a possible round-up, ask different groups what they found out in their interviews.

5.8 TOP DOGS

Listening 📼

This is a Listening Comprehension Passage. For procedure see 'Dealing with listening' in Part 3.

Leyton Towers, the high-rise block of flats in the city's West End, recently changed its long-standing rules about pets. The council decided last February to let the residents keep animals in the flats, and Mrs Nora Compton was one of the first residents to take the opportunity to have pets. She spoke to our reporter, Clive Williams, about her dogs.

Reporter: How long have you been interested in dogs?

Mrs Compton: Well I've always liked dogs ever since I was a kid I suppose, and I've had dogs of my own on and off for, oh, 20 years now.

Reporter: And now you have one dog, two dogs?

Mrs Compton: I've got two dogs and a cat.

Reporter: And this is in a small flat.

Mrs Compton: Well it's not all that small but it is a flat without a garden and it's on the sixth floor.

Reporter: You also have a full-time job – don't you find it very time-consuming looking after the dogs?

Mrs Compton: No, not if you like doing it, like everything else it is time-consuming but it's no bother if you like doing it.

Reporter: How much time do you spend every day looking after the dogs?

Mrs Compton: I spend at least two hours a day, because you have to take them out for walks at least four times a day and then there's feeding them and combing them and cleaning them – so it's at least two hours.

Reporter: And if you get a dog as a puppy you have to train it obviously to live indoors.

Mrs Compton: Well yes especially if you're living in a flat because the dog has to be very very clean and of course he has to be trained to do his business outside, and that takes a lot of training at the beginning and a lot of patience.

Reporter: How exactly do you go about training a dog? What do you have to do?

61

Mrs Compton: Well you see when he's a puppy the moment you see signs that he might pee, which is usually after eating, you try to make an area covered with newspaper and rush the dog there so that eventually he will see that and start using the newspaper. You have to do this because you can't take the dog out until he's vaccinated which is after he's three months old. Now when he's vaccinated you can train him to go outside and do it, but of course he's got used to the newspaper so at first you'll probably have to take some newspaper outside too and put it on the ground you see ...

Reporter: I see, so it doesn't take very long to get them used to the idea?

Mrs Compton: Well it all depends on the type of dog. Sometimes you can train a dog in a few months but with the two I've got it took quite a lot longer, about six months altogether I suppose – but it really depends on the type of dog.

Reporter: So you're living in this high-rise block with dogs. Did it take the neighbours very long for them to get used to the idea that there were two large dogs living next door?

Mrs Compton: Well it did take a bit of time yes, but really it was the kids round here that helped them to get over that – they all really like our dogs and now a lot of them are even trying to get their parents to have one too.

Reporter: I suppose you could say it's quite good for security too.

Mrs Compton: Yes that's funny but you see now because the kids have been putting pressure on their parents, the parents seem to be coming round to the idea too, so now they're all going round saying what a good idea it is because it'll stop muggers and vandals and people like that coming into our block of flats – and we've all been trying to do something about that for a long time.

Answers: (1) (a) They have been in existence for a long time.
     (b) They let the residents keep pets in their flats.
(2) (a) F (b) T (c) T (d) T
(3) Time-consuming = it takes up a lot of time.
    No bother = she doesn't mind doing it.
(4) Take them for walks, feed them, comb them, clean them.
(5) The dog has to be very clean; it has to 'do its business' outside.
(6) (See transcript.)
(7) (a) They were suspicious.
    (b) The children liked the dogs.
    (c) They think it's a good idea; it keeps muggers and vandals away.

Writing

The writing can be done immediately after answering the comprehension questions, or can be left for homework. In either case, students should prepare for the writing by taking notes from the tape on house-training a puppy.

Activities (following Unit 5)

CARICATURES

> **Language:** This activity draws on language from:
> Unit 2 (Appearance)
> Unit 4 (Attitudes and reactions)
> and also Intermediate units concerned with
> Comparison and Explanation. (See Table 1
> on p.3.)

1 Either discuss the questions with the whole class, or let them discuss them in groups and ask them to report their conclusions afterwards. Photographs and cartoons of local personalities can also of course be used.
2 The writing can be done in class or for homework.

COMPOSITION

> **Language:** Compositions (1) and (2) can be approached
> in various ways. Composition (3) is a written
> extension of 4.8.

The writing can be done in class or for homework.

Unit 6   Reporting

This is one of a series of units concerned with *narration* of past events. It deals with language for reporting what people said and thought.

The unit falls into two sections, followed by a Free Writing exercise and a Reading Comprehension. Both sections are concerned with reporting conversations. The first section practises basic reported speech structures; the second section focusses on particular verbs used in reporting.

Assumed knowledge

Before beginning this unit, students should be familiar with:

Past and Past Perfect tenses (Intermediate Units 12, 22, Upper-Intermediate Unit 3).

Basic structures for reporting requests, offers and advice (Intermediate Units 7, 14).

6.1 REPORTED SPEECH
Presentation of: reported speech structures.
Practice

6.2 CONFLICTING REPORTS
Practice

6.3 FORTUNE-TELLING
Free practice

6.4 KINDS OF STATEMENT
Presentation and practice of: verbs for reporting statements.
Practice

6.5 INFLUENCING AND TAKING ACTION
Presentation and practice of: other reporting verbs.

6.6 CONVER-SATIONS
Free practice

6.7 SMOOTH TALKING
Writing

6.8 MURDER!
Reading
Discussion
Writing

6.1 REPORTED SPEECH

> **Language:** Basic tense changes involved in reported speech.

Presentation

1 Read the texts. Ask students to re-construct what the two people actually
   said. The purpose of this is to focus attention on the tense changes.
   Note: The purpose of reported speech is to report the *content* of what was
   said. So the words used in the 'report' may be the same as those the speaker
   used, but don't have to be. The speakers in A and B may have used the
   actual words reported, or may have said the same things in a different way.
2 Ask students to tell you the basic changes that take place in reported speech.
   Build up this table on the board:

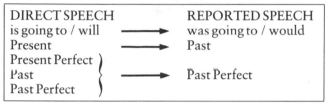

DIRECT SPEECH	REPORTED SPEECH
is going to / will ⟶	was going to / would
Present ⟶	Past
Present Perfect ⎫	
Past ⎬ ⟶	Past Perfect
Past Perfect ⎭	

Point out that these changes are made because what is being reported is *set
in the past*; the reporting verb (*said* / *told me*) is in the past, so what follows
must change 'one tense back':
Direct Speech: 'I*'m* from Australia'.
Indirect Speech: He *says* he*'s* from Australia.
Reported Speech: He *said* he *was* from Australia.
Note: It is sometimes unnecessary to change the tense in reported speech
(e.g. when reporting statements that are generally true or still valid) – but it
is never wrong to make the tense change.

Practice

Ask students to report the remarks round the class. Each time they should
begin *He said...* or *He told me...*
▶ W6 Ex 1 ◀

6.2 CONFLICTING REPORTS   Practice

> **Language:** Practice of language introduced in 6.1.
>
> *Note:* This exercise concentrates on a very common use of
> reported speech: to show surprise when things seem to
> conflict with what was said earlier.
> It includes 'reported thought' structures using:
> *I thought..., I didn't know..., I didn't realise...*

1 Do the first part of the exercise with the whole class.
    Possible continuations: (1) ...you weren't hungry.
                                    (2) ...it was going to be sunny.
                                    (3) ...it was only £20 a week.
                                    (4) ...you'd given up smoking.
                                    (5) ...anyone could bathe here.
                                    (6) ...you were keeping this evening free.
                                    (7) ...you wanted to come.
2 ▭ Play the example on the tape. If you think it is necessary, demonstrate the groupwork by doing the first item with the whole class.
3 Divide the class into groups for the activity.
▶ W6 Ex 2 ◀

6.3 FORTUNE-TELLING   Free practice

> **Language:** Free practice of language introduced so far in this unit.

1 Choose one person from each group to be fortune-tellers, or ask for volunteers. Provide a place for them to sit apart from the others.
2 One person from each group goes to have his fortune told. While they are waiting, the others can think of questions they might ask the fortune-teller.
3 The second person from each group goes to have his fortune told. Meanwhile, the first person tells the others what the fortune-teller told him. Continue in the same way until everyone has had his fortune told and has reported it to the rest of the group.

6.4 KINDS OF STATEMENT

> **Language:** Special verbs for reporting statements.

Presentation and practice ▭

This is a Listening Presentation. (See 'Dealing with listening' in Part 3.)

Woman: Two months ago, Mr Jim Lock, of Kimberley Road, Croydon, received a visit from a salesman representing Bargain Electrics Ltd, who persuaded him to buy an electric drill for £60. He told Mr Lock that if he sent a £15 deposit, they would send him the drill on a two-week home trial. If, after that time, he didn't want to keep the drill, he should send it back and his deposit would be refunded. The salesman assured Mr Lock that he was under no obligation to buy the drill if he didn't like it.

Man: Mr Lock sent his deposit and received the drill a few days later. But when he tried it out he found it didn't work, and the same afternoon his wife saw exactly the same drill in a local shop for only £50.

Woman: So he sent the drill back to Bargain Electrics with a letter. In the letter he explained that he didn't want the drill because it didn't work, and pointed out that the same drill could be bought locally for £10 less.

Man: Instead of getting his deposit back, as he expected, Mr Lock got a letter from Bargain Electrics in which they claimed that he had broken the drill by using it wrongly, and that he still owed them £45.

Woman: So Mr Lock wrote back to them. He strongly denied that he had broken the drill, and asked them again to return his £15.

Man: A few days later he got a letter from the Managing Director, who insisted that the drill had reached Mr Lock in perfect condition, and warned him that if he didn't pay the balance within seven days, the company would have to take legal action.

Woman: At this point, Mr Lock contacted us, and we phoned Bargain Electrics. We spoke to the Sales Manager, who at first accused us of interfering in a private matter, but eventually agreed to have the drill inspected.

Man: The next morning we had a very polite phone call from the Managing Director himself, who admitted that Mr Lock had been right all along, and that the drill had been wrongly assembled in the factory.

Woman: And we're pleased to say that the very next day Mr Lock received his £15 deposit – and a new drill. He assures us that the new drill works perfectly.

1 Play the tape. Students answer the questions, which check general comprehension.

Answers: (1) It's a 'consumer protection' programme to expose firms, etc. who have cheated customers or treated them badly.
   (2) He was under no obligation to buy it, and could try it out for two weeks then send it back if he didn't like it.
   (3) He found it didn't work; his wife saw the same drill being sold cheaper.
   (4) (a) He should get his £15 deposit back. (b) He should pay them £45.
   (5) 'Safeguard' phoned Bargain Electrics; the Sales Manager agreed to have the drill inspected; the Managing Director admitted the drill was faulty; Mr Lock got a new drill and his deposit back.

2 Look at the list of verbs. Ask students to tell you how they might be used to talk about the situation on the tape.

Write them on the board in these groups to show differences in structure:

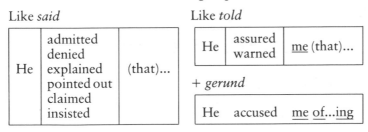

Like *said*

He	admitted denied explained pointed out claimed insisted	(that)...

Like *told*

He	assured warned	me (that)...

+ *gerund*

He	accused	me of...ing

3 Play the tape again. Students listen without writing anything down. After they have heard it, they try to complete the sentences using verbs from the list.

4 Go through the answers.

Practice

Divide the class into pairs. The interviews should be based on the information on the tape, but the students can of course add any details they like.

▶ W6 Ex 3 ◀

6.5   INFLUENCING AND   Presentation and practice
TAKING ACTION

> **Language:** Special verbs for reporting remarks in which:
> i)   the speaker tried to make the other person
>   do something (e.g. *advised, insisted*) or
> ii) said he would do something himself (e.g.
>   *promised, threatened*).

1 Look at the list of verbs and check that students understand what they
   mean. Ask students to use each one in a sentence of their own.
   Build up these groups on the board to show differences in structure:

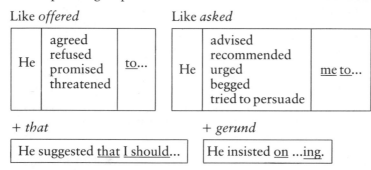

Like *offered*

| He | agreed
refused
promised
threatened | to... |

Like *asked*

| He | advised
recommended
urged
begged
tried to persuade | me to... |

+ *that*

| He suggested <u>that</u> I should... |

+ *gerund*

| He insisted <u>on</u> ...ing. |

2 🔊   Play the remarks on the tape. Then divide the class into groups to
   discuss the remarks and report them.
3 Go through the answers.
   Note: Students should report the *meaning* of what was said, and not
   attempt to reproduce the exact words. So the answer to (1) is simply: 'The
   salesman urged / tried to persuade Mr Lock to buy the drill'.
   ▶ W6 Ex 4 ◀

6.6   CONVERSATIONS   Free practice

> **Language:** Free practice of language introduced in this
>   unit.

1 Demonstrate the groupwork by reporting a conversation you remember
   yourself. Bring in reported speech structures and reporting verbs wherever
   they are appropriate.
2 Divide the class into groups for the activity.
3 As a round-up, ask each group to tell their most interesting story to the rest
   of the class.
   ▶ W6 Ex 5 ◀

6.7 SMOOTH TALKING   Writing

> **Language:** Free practice of language introduced in this unit.

1 As a preparation for the writing, look at the story outlines with the class, and ask students to tell each story orally.
Note: The illustrations provide the key points in the story only; other details of the stories are deliberately left open to the imagination. Encourage students to expand each story with details of their own.
2 The writing can be done in class or for homework.

6.8 MURDER!

Reading

For procedure see 'Dealing with reading' in Part 3.
Answers: (1) (a) If George was married, he would get half of his father's fortune, and Lady Forbes would get the other half. If not, Lady Forbes would get it all.
(b) He wanted to encourage his son to get married and settle down.
(2) (a) She had had an affair with the chauffeur, Grimes.
(b) Because if Sir Clarence had known, he would have stopped the wedding.
(c) She wanted Sir Clarence to know, because if the wedding was cancelled she would get all her husband's fortune.
(3) (a) The gun in her hand, and the suicide note.
(b) The gun was in the wrong hand, and the note was in the wrong hand-writing.
(4) (a) She thought her plan (to tell Sir Clarence about the affair with Grimes) would not work, so she murdered Anna to stop the wedding from taking place.
(b) There is no reason for her to have thought that her plan would not work. In fact Lestrade says that 'there is no doubt Sir Clarence would have stopped the wedding if he had known'.
(5) George didn't have an alibi. The other two were out in the car.
(6) (a) ...of murdering Anna Young / of murder.
(b) ...murdering her / that she had murdered her.
(c) ...to tell Sir Clarence about the affair.
(d) ...that she had heard the shot while she was (had been) in the bath.
(7) Because he couldn't understand how Holmes knew.
Because he couldn't see the relevance of the question.

Discussion

This is best conducted in groups, followed by a round-up with the whole class.

Writing

The writing can be done in class or for homework. Students should do the writing before they read the confession on page 165 of their books.

Activities (following Unit 6)

SHORTLIST

> **Language:** This activity draws on language from:
> Unit 1 (Experience)
> Unit 5 (Duration)
> and also Intermediate units concerned with
> Personal information and Past and present.
> (See Table 1 on p.3.)

1 Choose four students to be the applicants. Divide the rest of the class into four groups, each group representing a package tour company. The applicants prepare individually, the interview boards prepare in their groups.
2 Each of the applicants is interviewed by the four boards in turn.
3 Ask each board and each applicant who they have chosen and why.

COMPOSITION

> **Language:** Composition (1) can be approached in various ways, and covers no specific language areas; Compositions (2) and (3) draw on the same language as the previous activity.

The writing can be done in class or for homework.

SITUATIONS

> **Language:** The situations draw on language from Units 4, 5 and 6.

For procedure, see Activities following Unit 3.

Unit 7 Deductions and explanations

This is one of a series of units concerned with *explanation* and speculation about the past, present and future. It deals with language for making deductions and explaining the significance of things.

The unit falls into three sections followed by a Reading Comprehension. The first two sections are concerned with making deductions and giving reasons for deductions. The first section practises the modal verbs *must, may, might* and *can't* followed by present and past infinitives; the second section shows the relationship between these verbs and conditional structures with *If*. The third section is concerned with explaining the significance of situations and events, and practises a range of appropriate verbs.

Assumed knowledge

Before beginning this unit, students should be familiar with:
Present and past infinitive forms (Intermediate Unit 23, Upper-Intermediate Unit 2).
Conditional structures (Intermediate Unit 23).

7.1 MUST, MIGHT, MAY & CAN'T
Presentation of: must, might, may, can't + infinitive forms.

7.2 WORKING IT OUT
Practice

7.3 WHAT'S GOING ON?
Practice

7.4 DEDUCTIONS AND REASONS: 'IF'
Presentation of: If + Past and Past Perfect tenses.
Practice

7.5 OUT OF THIS WORLD
Free practice

7.6 EXPLA-NATIONS
Practice of: indicate/mean/suggest that.
Writing

7.7 PERSONALITY QUIZ
Free practice

7.8 OUT OF THE BLUE
Reading
Writing

7.1 MUST, MIGHT, MAY & CAN'T   Presentation 🎦

> **Language:** Use of modals for making deductions: *must,*
> *may/might, can't* + present and past
> infinitives.

This is a Listening Presentation. (See 'Dealing with listening' in Part 3.)

Dialogue 1
A: Poor old George. Fancy having an awful job like that. They must pay him well.
B: Oh, I don't know. He can't earn much – look at that old car he drives.
A: That doesn't prove anything – he might enjoy driving an old car.
B: Maybe, but he can't enjoy wearing that dreadful old suit of his.
A: Mm, that's true. Well, in that case, why doesn't he resign?

Dialogue 2
A: Is Hilda here?
B: No, it's her lunch hour. Try the canteen – she may be having a snack with Jimmy.
A: No, she isn't – I've just come from there.
B: Hm. She must have gone out to a restaurant, then.
A: Well she can't have gone far – her coat's still here.
B: Ah, in that case she might be having a curry at the Taj Mahal – it's only round the corner.

Dialogue 3
A: It's obvious what happened. He must have been sitting in bed smoking the pipe. Then he fell asleep and dropped the pipe, which set fire to the bedclothes, and he was suffocated by the smoke.
B: Ah but there are two things you don't know. First he can't have been smoking the pipe – he gave up smoking at least a year ago...
A: He might have started again!
B: Second, when his lungs were examined, there was no trace of smoke in them. So he must have stopped breathing *before* the fire started...

1 Play Dialogue 1 and check general comprehension by asking questions:
   e.g. What kind of job does George have?
         What's his car like?
         What kind of clothes does he wear?
2 Play the dialogue again. Students write what the man and woman say. Go through the answers.
3 Repeat the procedure with Dialogues 2 and 3.
4 As you go through the answers:
   i) Establish what the different modal verbs mean:
       He *must* be rich = I'm sure he's rich.
       He *may/might* be rich = Perhaps he's rich.
       He *may/might* not be rich = Perhaps he isn't rich.
       He *can't* be rich = I'm sure he isn't rich.
   ii) Establish that modals are followed by infinitive (without *to*). Point out

that there are *four* possible infinitive forms. Write this table on the board to show how they relate to different tenses:

PRESENT
I'm sure he work<u>s</u> hard. ⟶ He must <u>work</u> hard.
I'm sure he'<u>s</u> work<u>ing</u> hard. ⟶ He must <u>be</u> working hard.

PAST
I'm sure ⎪ he work<u>ed</u> / he <u>has</u> work<u>ed</u> ⎪ hard. ⟶ He must <u>have</u> work<u>ed</u> hard.
I'm sure ⎪ he <u>was</u> working / he'<u>s</u> <u>been</u> work<u>ing</u> ⎪ hard. ⟶ He must <u>have</u> <u>been</u> work<u>ing</u> hard.

5 Ask students to change the sentences round the class.
▶ **W7 Ex 1** ◀

7.2 WORKING IT OUT   Practice

> **Language:** Practice of language introduced in 7.1.

1 Either read out the questions yourself and ask students to answer them round the class, or let students do the exercise in pairs and go through the answers afterwards.
2 Divide the class into pairs for the second part of the exercise. They should think of as many different continuations as they can.
3 Ask different pairs what continuations they thought of.
▶ **W7 Ex 2** ◀

7.3 WHAT'S GOING ON?   Practice

> **Language:** Further practice of language introduced in 7.1.

1 Look at the first picture with the whole class. In answering the questions, students should use *must, might* or *can't*, and give a reason:
   e.g. (1) They can't be father and daughter, because there isn't enough difference between their ages.
2 Students discuss the other two pictures in groups.
3 Go through the questions, and ask different groups what conclusions they came to.

7.4 DEDUCTIONS AND REASONS: 'IF'

> **Language:** Further practice of language introduced in 7.1.
> Conditional sentences with *If....*, used in giving reasons for a deduction ('Second', 'Third' and 'Mixed' Conditionals).

Presentation

1 🔊 Play the two monologues on the tape, and let students follow in their books. Check that students understand what each one is about.
2 Use the answers to the questions to build up a presentation of *If* sentences on the board, getting suggestions from the class as much as possible:

Referring to the present

> They <u>can't be</u> car lights, because they <u>are</u> different colours.
> → If they <u>were</u> car lights, they <u>would</u> be all white.

Referring to the past

> He <u>can't have</u> liv<u>ed</u> in Cyprus, because he <u>didn't</u> understand the waiter.
> → If he <u>had</u> liv<u>ed</u> in Cyprus, he <u>would have</u> understood the waiter.

'Mixed'

> <u>Present/Past</u>: He <u>can't be</u> a doctor, because he <u>didn't</u> know what hepatitis was.
> → If he <u>was</u> a doctor, he <u>would have</u> known what hepatitis was.
> <u>Past/Present</u>: He <u>must have</u> been to America, because he <u>has</u> a US stamp in his passport.
> → If he <u>hadn't been</u> to America, he <u>wouldn't</u> have a US stamp in his passport.

Practice

1 🔊 Play the example on the tape. Demonstrate the pairwork by doing (1) with the whole class.
2 Divide the class into groups to do the exercise.
3 As a possible round-up, ask different groups what reasons they thought of.
▶ W7 Ex 3, Ex 4 ◀

7.5 OUT OF THIS WORLD   Free practice

> **Language:** Free practice of language introduced so far in this unit.

1 Divide the class into three (or six) groups. Give each group a different topic to discuss.
2 Ask one person from each group to say what conclusions they came to about their topic, and why. If you like, this can be broadened out into a general class discussion at this point.

7.6 EXPLANATIONS

> **Language:** Expressions for talking about the meaning or
> significance of facts:
> *indicates/means/suggests that...*
> *doesn't necessarily mean that...*

Practice 🖭

This exercise begins with a Listening Model. (See 'Dealing with listening' in
Part 3.)

About seven out of ten people released
from prison end up in prison again
sooner or later. A lot of people think
this simply indicates that once a person
becomes a criminal he will probably
remain a criminal. But of course it
doesn't necessarily mean that at all. On
the contrary, it could equally suggest
that being in prison actually makes
people more likely to commit crimes.
After all, prisons are full of criminals,
and this means that someone going to
prison for the first time is going to meet
a lot more criminals than he's met
before. So he'll probably learn a lot
about crime during his stay there. The
fact that so many people get re-arrested
also suggests that prisons aren't doing
enough to train people for jobs they can
do when they get out. If they were given
this training, ex-prisoners wouldn't need
to turn to crime again to make a living.

1 Play the tape. Students answer questions (1)–(3).
2 Make sure students understand these expressions:

> indicates/means/suggests that...
> doesn't necessarily mean that...
> may indicate / could suggest that...

3 Discuss (4) with the class.
4 Divide the class into groups to discuss the other topics.
5 Ask each group what conclusions they came to, and why.

Writing

The writing can be done in class or for homework.
► W7 Ex 5 ◄

7.7 PERSONALITY QUIZ   Free practice

> **Language:** Free practice of language introduced in 7.6.
> Practice of 'character' vocabulary introduced in
> 4.7.

1 Give time for students to go through the quiz individually and mark their
answers.

2 Before the next stage, do some quick revision of relevant vocabulary,
   e.g. sociable/unsociable, introvert/extrovert, outgoing/reserved/shy,
      sensitive/insensitive, mean/generous, considerate/inconsiderate.
3 Divide the class into pairs. Each student gives the quiz he has filled in to his
   partner, who goes through his answers and interprets them.
4 Ask individual students to make general comments about their partner's
   personality, as indicated by the quiz.

7.8 OUT OF THE BLUE

Reading

For procedure, see 'Dealing with reading' in Part 3.

Answers: (1) Large ice-blocks falling from the sky.
   (2) That it can't have been a hailstone.
      That it can't have dropped from a plane.
   (3) (a) That they are hailstones, or ice somehow produced by weather
         conditions.
         That they come from space.
         That they drop from planes.
      (b) The Drexel Institute says that they are not.
         They would probably melt when entering the Earth's atmosphere.
         De-icing equipment prevents ice forming on planes. Also this
         would not explain those which fell before planes existed.
   (4) (a) That water had leaked from a plane, frozen and dropped off.
      (b) (i) If there had been a plane overhead, the people would have seen
            it.
         (ii) If the ice-blocks had fallen from a plane 20 seconds apart, they
            would have landed miles from each other, not almost in the
            same place.
   (5) (a) This fall was significant because it was witnessed by a reputable
         scientist; because it was *kept* and analysed.
      (b) Because of the strange fact that there were *two* blocks of ice, one
         after the other. This demonstrates the inadequacy of the airplane
         theory.
   (6) (This is a discussion question.)

Writing

This section gives practice in summary writing. The writing can be done
immediately after answering the comprehension questions, or can be left for
homework.

Activities (following Unit 7)

OUT AND ABOUT

> **Language:** This activity draws on language from:
> Unit 1 (Experience)
> Unit 4 (Attitudes and reactions)
> Unit 5 (Duration)
> and also Intermediate units concerned with
> Description and Comparison. (See Table 1
> on p.3.)

1 Either prepare a list of suitable places/services before the lesson, or let each
pair choose their own, making sure that they are all different. They should
of course all be familiar enough for most of the class to be able to express an
attitude towards them.
Note: If you are teaching a mixed-nationality class in Britain, you could use
an alternative list of topics covering aspects of life in Britain (e.g. British
food, train services, drivers, houses).
2 Give time for each pair to work out what questions they will ask.
3 If you have enough space, let students wander freely round the class (in
pairs, with one student acting as 'secretary') and interview whoever they
like.
4 After the activity, give a few minutes for each pair to 'collate' their information before asking them to summarise it to the rest of the class.

COMPOSITION

> **Language:** The composition draws on the same language
> areas as Activity 1 and may also include
> 'reporting' language (Unit 6).

The writing can be done in class or for homework.

Unit 8   Advantages and disadvantages

This is one of a series of units concerned with *comparison* and evaluation. It deals with ways of talking about advantages and disadvantages and discussing possible courses of action.

The unit falls into three sections, followed by a Reading Comprehension. The first section is concerned with good and bad effects; it practises a range of 'effect' verbs and special structures for talking about advantages and disadvantages. The second section is concerned with the advantages and disadvantages of a particular course of action, and practises structures for giving advice. The third section is concerned with discussing the consequences of different courses of action, and practises conditional structures with *If*.

Assumed knowledge

Before beginning this unit, students should be familiar with:
Infinitives and gerunds.
Basic advice structures (Intermediate Unit 14).
Conditional structures (Intermediate Unit 23,
  Upper-Intermediate Unit 7).

8.1 GOOD AND BAD EFFECTS
Presentation of: 'Effect' verbs.
Practice

8.2 PROS AND CONS
Practice

8.3 ADVANTAGES AND DISADVANTAGES
Presentation of:
(dis)advantage of /
drawback of / good
(bad) thing about /
trouble with.
Free practice
Writing

8.4 COURSES OF ACTION
Presentation and practice of: ought to, ought not to, there's no point in, might as well.

8.5 ADVISING ON A CHOICE
Practice

8.6 DON'T DO IT: READING GAME
Practice

8.7 WHAT WOULD HAPPEN?
Presentation and practice of: If +
Present tense... will...;
If + Past tense...
would...
Free practice
Writing

8.8 DISHWASHERS
Reading
Writing

8.1 GOOD AND BAD EFFECTS

> **Language:** Verbs for describing the effect things have on what people do:
> i) with infinitive structures (e.g. *enable...to...*)
> ii) with gerund structures (e.g. *prevent...from + -ing*).

Presentation 📼

This is a Listening Presentation. (See 'Dealing with listening' in Part 3.)

The inhabitants of Tango, a small island in the South Pacific, discovered a plant which contained a powerful drug. This drug made it more difficult for them to think rationally – it stopped them worrying about the future, and enabled them to forget all their problems. At the same time, it made it much easier for them to relax and enjoy themselves: so much so, indeed, that the whole population of the island stopped working and spent all their time singing and dancing and looking at the sea.

Unfortunately this had a very bad effect on the country's economy, and people began to run short of food. This, however didn't discourage the people from taking the drug. The Prime Minister made speeches on the TV warning them about the drug, but nobody took any notice, and before long the economy was in ruins.

This forced the Government to make the drug illegal. But that only made the situation worse. The law couldn't prevent the people from taking the drug, which grew wild all over the island; on the contrary, the fact that the drug was illegal merely encouraged people to take it.

Eventually, the Government found a better solution: they exported the drug to other countries. This saved the islanders from having to work more than one day a week, and allowed them to spend the rest of their time sitting in the sun without a care in the world.

1 Play the tape. Students answer the questions, which check general comprehension.
  Note: It is not important at this stage that students use the 'target' verbs in their answers. An adequate answer to (1) would be 'When they took the drug, they forgot their problems and stopped worrying about the future'.
2 Play the tape again, and tell the class to listen out for the verbs in the list, but not to write anything down. After the text is finished, ask the class to complete the sentences using verbs from the list.
3 Go through the answers. As you do so, write the structures on the board in groups, eliciting as much information from the students as you can:

+ infinitive

enable allow encourage force	someone	<u>to</u> do something

make it	easier more difficult	(for someone) <u>to</u> do something

+ gerund

stop prevent save	someone	(<u>from</u>) do<u>ing</u> something
discourage	someone	<u>from</u> do<u>ing</u> something

4 Point out the relationship between some of these verbs and modals:

i) It | enables / allows | them to work – they *can* work.

ii) It | stops / prevents | them (from) working – they *can't* work.

iii) It forces them to work – they *have* to work.

iv) It saves them (from) working – they *don't have to* work.

Practice

Divide the class into pairs. Each pair improvises an interview based on the information they heard on the tape, but adding any details they like.
Note: In this part of the exercise, students use the verbs introduced above, but in the *Present tense*. This is a preparation for the exercises that follow.

8.2 PROS AND CONS Practice

> **Language:** Practice of language introduced in 8.1, for talking in general about advantages and disadvantages.

1 🔊 Play the example on the tape. Ask students to suggest other advantages and disadvantages of package holidays.
2 Divide the class into groups to discuss the other topics.
3 As a round-up, ask different groups what they said about each topic.
   ► W8 Ex 1 ◄

8.3 ADVANTAGES AND DISADVANTAGES

> **Language:** Structures used for listing or 'weighing up' advantages and disadvantages using:
> *(dis)advantage of..., drawback of..., good/bad thing about..., trouble with...*
> Practice of language introduced in 8.1.

Presentation

1 Read the text. Students answer (1).
2 Look at the list of words in (2), and ask students to tell you how the writer uses them in the text. If necessary, build up this table on the board to show the range of structures:

The One The main Another	(dis) advantage <u>of</u> good/bad thing <u>about</u> drawback <u>of</u>	being unemployed is that...
The (main) trouble <u>with</u>		

Point out that:
i) 'Drawback' = a minor disadvantage of something that is otherwise good.
ii) You can only say '*the* trouble' (not '*a* trouble').
3 Ask students to give their own opinion of being unemployed, using the structures you have presented.

Free practice

1 Divide the class into groups for the discussion.
2 As a round-up, ask one person from each group to report their conclusions to the whole class.

Writing

The writing can be done in class or for homework.
▶ W8 Ex 2, Ex 5 ◀

8.4 COURSES OF ACTION   Presentation and practice

> **Language:** Structures for advising on a course of action, in terms of its advantages/disadvantages: *ought to, ought not to, there's no point in, might as well.*

1 Look at the captions, and establish what the structures mean by asking students to match them with (1) (a) (b) (c) and (d).
   Answers: (a) ought to;   (b) ought not to;   (c) there's no point in;   (d) might as well.
   Point out these structures:
   (*We*) *might as well* + infinitive (without *to*)
   There's no point in + noun or gerund

2 As a possible extension, you could ask students to suggest reasons the people in the cartoons might give for each of their remarks:
   e.g. We ought to vote Liberal because they have a good foreign policy.
   We might as well vote Liberal – they're bound to win anyway.
   We ought not to take the car – the roads are icy.
   There's no point in taking the car as it's only a few minutes' walk.

3 Look at the example, and ask students to change the sentences round the class.

   Answers: (1) You ought not to...   (5) You might as well...
             (2) There's no point in...   (6) You ought to...
             (3) We might as well...   (7) We ought not to...
             (4) There's no point in...   (8) There's no point in...

8.5 ADVISING ON A CHOICE   Practice

> **Language:** Practice of:
>   i) *might as well*, and *There's no point in* + *-ing*
>   ii) *It's not worth* + *-ing.*

1 📼 Play the example on the tape. Point out that *It's not worth doing* is an alternative to *There's no point in doing.*
2 Demonstrate the groupwork by doing (1) with the whole class.
3 Divide the class into groups of three to do the exercise.
4 As a possible round-up, ask students what they decided they might as well do in each case.
   ▶ W8 Ex 3 ◀

8.6 DON'T DO IT : READING GAME   Practice

> **Language:** Structures for advising against an action:
>   i) *You'd better not...* (see Intermediate Unit 14)
>   ii) *There's no point in* + *-ing* and *It's no use* + *-ing.*
>
> *Note:* There is a slight difference in meaning between *It's not worth doing* (8.5) and *It's no use doing*:
> e.g. *It's not worth* taking the lift – he only lives on the second floor (=we could take the lift, but there's no advantage in doing so).
> *It's no use* taking the lift – it's broken down (=trying to take the lift won't get us anywhere).
> *There's no point in doing* covers both these meanings.

1 Look at the examples. Point out that:
   i) *You'd better not* (+ infinitive without *to*) means the same as *You ought not to*, but is stronger and is used especially for warnings.

ii) *It's no use* + *-ing* means the same as *There's no point in* + *-ing* : that there is no advantage in a course of action, it won't do any good.

2 Divide the class into groups of three and give each student a letter: A, B or C.

3 Demonstrate the game by reading out Student A's sentence (1), changing it to:

'You'd better not pick up the gun...'

Ask Students B and C to look in their own section for a suitable continuation and read it out:

'...you'll get your fingerprints on it'.

Then read out Student A's sentence (1) again, changing it to:

'It's no use picking up the gun...'

Students B and C again look in their own sections for a suitable continuation:

'...it's not loaded'.

4 Give a few minutes for students to read through their own section silently. Answer any vocabulary questions.

5 Students play the game.

6 When most groups have finished, go through the answers with the class.

Answers: A: (1) (See above.)

(2) You'd better not run away: people will think you're guilty.
It's no use running away: they'll find you in no time.

(3) You'd better not lock the door: John may not have a key.
There's no point in locking the door: they've got skeleton keys.

B: (1) You'd better not wait for Mr Jenkins: you'll be late for the theatre.
There's no point in waiting for Mr Jenkins: he won't be back until tomorrow.

(2) You'd better not try to bribe him: he might report you to the police.
It's no use trying to bribe him: he's totally incorruptible.

(3) You'd better not ask him for a rise in salary: lots of people would like to have your job.
There's no point in asking him for a rise in salary: he's terribly stingy.

C: (1) You'd better not take those pills: they might poison you.
It's no use taking those pills: they won't have any effect.

(2) You'd better not punish him: his mother will complain.
It's no use punishing him: he doesn't know what he's done.

(3) You'd better not ask her how old she is: you'll probably offend her.
It's no use asking her how old she is: she hasn't even told her best friends.

8.7   WHAT WOULD HAPPEN?

> **Language:** Conditional structures, for weighing up
> possibilities in the future:
> i) *If* + Present ...*will...* ('First Conditional') for
> talking about real future plans.
> ii) *If* + Past...*would...* ('Second Conditional')
> for imagining alternative possibilities.
> Free practice of language introduced in this
> unit.

Presentation and practice

1 Read the text. Make sure students understand why the 'Second Conditional'
is used here. If necessary, give these examples:
  (i) If you *go* to university you *will* get a degree, and that *will* enable you to
  get a better job.
  – The speaker is *predicting* what will happen. He sees it as *real* – a
  definite plan for the future. (See Intermediate Unit 19.)
  (ii) If you *went* to university, you *would* get a degree, and that *would*
  enable you to get a better job.
  – The speaker is *imagining* what would happen. He sees it as just one of
  several possibilities for the future.
2 Ask students to comment on the other courses of action open to Sam.

Free practice

1 Demonstrate the groupwork by telling the class about a difficult choice of
your own, asking them to suggest things you could do.
2 Divide the class into groups for the activity.

Writing

The writing can be done in class or for homework.
► W8 Ex 4 ◄

8.8   DISHWASHERS

Reading

For procedure, see 'Dealing with reading' in Part 3.
Answers: (1) Possible answers:
  (a) He tells us how recent electrical appliances and other labour-saving
  devices have made housework easier.
  (b) He explains what kinds of dishwashers there are, what they do,
  and why they are useful.

    (c) He talks about some of the disadvantages of dishwashers.
 (2) Probably yes – he mentions the advantages of each labour-saving
      device, but none of the disadvantages.
 (3) Advantages: possible answers:
    (a) They will cook a meal for you while you are out.
    (b) They enable you to make toast while you are eating breakfast.
    (c) It's quick and it doesn't require any effort.
    (d) They save you having to hang your washing out to dry.
    Disadvantages: (This is a discussion question.)
 (4) (a) The basic jobs you have to do in the house.
    (b) The sky clouds over, and it's about to rain.
    (c) According to how much money you have.
    He thinks they are unusual – not things people normally make.
 (5) (a) T (b) F (c) F (d) T (e) F (f) T
 (6) Because the ones you have may not fit the machine.
    So that you only have to use the machine once a day.

Writing

This section gives practice in summary writing. It can be done immediately
after answering the comprehension questions, or can be left for homework.

Activities (following Unit 8)

SCANDAL

> **Language:** This activity draws on language from:
> Unit 4 (Attitudes and reactions)
> Unit 6 (Reporting)
> as well as Intermediate units concerned with
> Action and Comparison (See Table 1 on p.3.)

1 Read the newspaper article with the class, and present any new vocabulary.
2 Check comprehension by asking students to tell you what the article is about and what Lord Cramford's and Mrs Dickenson's views are.
3 Divide the class into three (or six) groups. Working together, they prepare what they will say.
4 Students form new groups, so that each group contains at least one person from each original group. They conduct the interview.
5 As a round-up, ask each group how their discussion developed.

COMPOSITION

> **Language:** The composition draws on the same language areas as the previous activity, and especially gives practice in reporting verbs (Unit 6).

The writing can be done in class or for homework.

Unit 9   Clarifying

This is one of a series of units concerned with *explanation* and speculation about the past, present and future. It deals with ways of asking for and checking information, correcting people, and reporting questions.

The unit falls into three sections, followed by a Listening Comprehension. The first section is concerned with asking for precise information, and practises more 'advanced' types of information questions and indirect question structures. The second section is concerned with checking on information and correcting other people; it practises tag questions and 'identifying' structures. The third section is concerned with reporting your own and other people's questions, and practises reported question structures.

Assumed knowledge

Before beginning this unit, students should be familiar with:
Structure of direct questions, using all tenses.
Formation of tag questions.
Reported speech structures (Upper-Intermediate Unit 6).

9.1 INFORMATION QUESTIONS
Presentation and practice of: information questions

9.2 GETTING FURTHER INFORMATION
Practice

9.3 INDIRECT QUESTIONS
Presentation of: indirect questions. Practice

9.4 WITNESS
Free practice

9.5 MAKING SURE
Presentation and practice of: tag questions and 'identifying' structures.

9.6 YOU'VE GOT IT ALL WRONG
Practice

9.7 REPORTED QUESTIONS
Presentation of: reported questions. Practice

9.8 UNDER FIRE
Free practice
Writing

9.9 JOB INTERVIEW
Listening
Free practice

9.1 INFORMATION QUESTIONS Presentation and practice

> **Language:** Questions for asking for precise information:
> i) *What kind of / sort of...?*
> *What size/colour/flavour...?*
> ii) Other question types using *How...?*
> *Which...? What...? How far...? How many...?*
> *Whose...?*

1 Either look at the picture, or introduce the exercise by setting the situation (with books closed) and eliciting the question 'Which way do we go?' If necessary, do some quick revision of basic question forms before you begin the exercise.

2 Do the exercise round the class. Present any new structures as you come to them. Insist on very *precise* questions:
e.g. (1) What flavour...?
Point out especially the difference between:
(8) What has he done *to* his leg? (= what damage has he done?) and
(11) What have you done *with* my football boots? (= where are they?).

3 The last part of the exercise provides a basis for vocabulary work on:
i) 'class' nouns, e.g. crime, rank, make, material, shade.
ii) particular examples of a class, e.g. different kinds of crime.
Discuss each of the sets, presenting new vocabulary as you go through the exercise, and ask students to make suitable information questions about each set.

Possible answers: (1) What crime did he commit?
(2) How shall I cook the meat?
(3) What rank was he promoted to?
(4) What kind of school are they at?
(5) What make of car was it?
(6) What material are the soles of your shoes made of?
(7) What size typing paper do you want?
(8) What shade of red is her dress?
(9) How would you like your steak done?
(10) What grade did he get in the test?
(Many answers possible.)

9.2 GETTING FURTHER INFORMATION Practice

> **Language:** Questions with a 'hanging preposition' for asking for further information:
> e.g. *What* are you thinking *about?*

1 ▭ Play the example on the tape. Point out that in his first question B is asking for further, more precise information. If necessary write these examples on the board to show how the questions are formed:

> He's doing something.
> <u>What</u> is he doing?

> I'm thinking about something.
> <u>What</u> are you thinking <u>about</u>?

2 Go through the exercise and establish what the other questions should be:
   e.g. (1) Who did she get engaged to?
       (2) What did he die of?
       (3) What are you going to wrap them in?
3 Students have conversations in pairs. They can continue the conversation in
   any way they like.
► W9 Ex 1 ◄

9.3 INDIRECT QUESTIONS

Presentation

> **Language:** Asking questions which include an *indirect*
> *question structure:*
> e.g. Do you know *where he went?*

1 Look at the examples and ask students to tell you the difference between the
   structures in each pair. Establish that:
   i) in normal direct questions the word order changes (inversion):

> He <u>went</u> somewhere.
> Where <u>did</u> he <u>go</u>?

   ii) In indirect questions the word order is the same as in an ordinary
       sentence:

Do you know Have you any idea Can you remember	<u>where he went</u>?

2 Either do the exercise round the class or let the students write the answers,
   working individually.

Practice

1 Demonstrate the groupwork by getting students to ask you a few questions
   about the three topics.
2 Students ask each other questions in groups.
► W9 Ex 2 ◄

9.4 WITNESS Free practice

> **Language:** Free practice of language introduced so far in
> this unit.
> Further practice of *might have been/done* (see
> Unit 7).

1 🔊 Play the witness's answers on the tape, and ask students to suggest
suitable questions.
Possible questions: Where exactly was he when you saw him?... Who was he
talking to?... What was the coat made of?... Did you notice what kind of
dog it was?... Can you remember how many of them there were?... What
happened next?... Do you know what kind of car it was?... What shade
of blue was it?

2 Divide the class into pairs. Make sure students understand what they have to
do, then give 30 seconds for one student from each pair to look at the picture.

3 One student in each pair tries to answer the other's questions.

9.5 MAKING SURE Presentation and practice

> **Language:** Use of tag questions and 'identifying structures'
> for checking on information:
> i) Simple tag questions:
> e.g. John gave us that book, *didn't he?*
> ii) Identifying clauses:
> e.g. John *was the person who* gave us that
> book, *wasn't he?*
> iii) Identifying clauses (beginning with *It*):
> e.g. *It was* John *who* gave us that book,
> *wasn't it?*

1 Write these sentences on the board:

> John gave us that book.
> We invited the Smiths.
> He left on Sunday.
> They met in London.

Look at the first sentence and tell the class that they think John gave us the
book, but they want to check. Ask them to make the sentence into a tag
question:

> John gave us that book, <u>didn't he?</u>

Elicit tag questions for the other sentences:
We invited the Smiths, didn't we?
He left on Sunday, didn't he?
They met in London, didn't they?

2 Establish that if you want to check that it was *John* and no one else you can say:

> John <u>was the person who</u> gave us that book, <u>wasn't he?</u>

Elicit similar questions for the other sentences:
   The Smiths were the people (who) we invited, weren't they?
   Sunday was the day (when) he left, wasn't it?
   London was the place where they met, wasn't it?
3 Establish that you can also say:

> <u>It was</u> John <u>who/that</u> gave us that book, <u>wasn't it?</u>

Elicit similar questions for the other sentences:
   It was the Smiths that we invited, wasn't it?
   It was on Sunday that he left, wasn't it?
   It was in London that they met, wasn't it?
4 🔲 Look at the picture, and play the examples on the tape. Then do the exercise round the class.
5 Play the pairwork example on the tape. Students have conversations in pairs.
▶ W9 Ex 3 ◀

9.6 YOU'VE GOT IT ALL WRONG   Practice 🔲

> **Language:** Practice of identifying clauses with *It...*, used
> for correcting people.
> Practice of tag questions.

This exercise begins with a Listening Model. (See 'Dealing with listening' in Part 3.)

1 Play the tape. Students answer the questions.
2 If you think it is necessary, demonstrate the groupwork by doing (1) with the whole class.
3 Students have similar conversations in groups of four, beginning with a tag question each time.
▶ W9 Ex 4 ◀

A: Richard bought a cassette recorder in Hong Kong, didn't he?
B: No, it wasn't Richard who bought it, it was Alan.
C: Anyway, it wasn't a cassette recorder that he bought, it was a radio.
D: Anyway, it wasn't in Hong Kong that he bought it, it was in Singapore.
A: I see – so Alan bought a radio in Singapore then. Is that right?

9.7 REPORTED QUESTIONS

> **Language:** Tense and word order changes involved in
> reported questions.

Presentation

1 Read the text, and establish what the speaker is talking about.
  Answer: coming through British immigration control.
2 Students re-construct what actual questions were asked:
  e.g. 'Have you ever visited Britain before?'
3 Point out that:
  i) The same rules for tense changes apply as for Reported speech (see Unit
      6.1). As in Reported speech, the question being reported is *set in the past*
      – the reporting verb (*asked me / wanted to know*) is in the past, so what
      follows must change 'one tense back'.
  ii) Reported questions, like Indirect questions, have the same word order as
      a normal sentence.
  Show how these structures are related by writing these examples on the
  board:

> Direct Question: <u>Does</u> he <u>like</u> cheese?
> Indirect Question: Do you know <u>if</u> he <u>likes</u> cheese?
> Reported Question: She ask<u>ed</u> me if he lik<u>ed</u> cheese.

Practice

(1) Look at the three groups of questions, and establish who might have asked
    them and on what occasions.
    Possible answers: 1st group: Asked by landlady or friend, for example, as soon as
        the speaker arrived.
        2nd group: Asked by doctor when the speaker went for a check-up.
        3rd group: Asked by owner/manager of restaurant, interviewing the
        speaker for a job.
(2) Ask students to report the questions round the class:
    e.g. The landlady asked me if I'd had a good journey.
▶ W9 Ex 5 ◀

9.8 UNDER FIRE

> **Language:** Free practice of language introduced in 9.7.

Free practice

1 Demonstrate the groupwork by telling the class about an occasion when
  you had to answer questions yourself.
2 Divide the class into groups for the activity.
3 As a possible round-up, ask each group to tell their most interesting story to
  the rest of the class.

Writing

The writing can be done in class or for homework.

9.9 JOB INTERVIEW

Listening 📼

This is a Listening Comprehension Passage. For procedure, see 'Dealing with listening' in Part 3.

Man: So how did the interview go?

Woman: It turned out very well. I thought it was going to be this formal interview but as it turned out I just went along and met the television producer and he took me out for lunch.

Man: Really? What did he ask you about?

Woman: Well he asked me, um – about what I'd done before and the jobs I'd had before and whether I'd got a degree and – just about my qualifications and things like that. And, and then he got on to asking me about the documentaries themselves and whether I'd be interested in doing the kind of research that was involved.

Man: So what did you say?

Woman: Well I said yes obviously I was fairly interested in energy, um because I'd spent a lot of time last year in fact going round places finding out about various different kinds of energy, and I'd been to a centre for alternative technology for example and I'd spent some time there finding out about wind power and solar power and things like that.

Man: Yeah, what are they about then, these documentaries?

Woman: Well they're going to cover all kinds of – of energy sources and the idea is that in six documentaries they'll look at oil and coal and nuclear energy, and then they'll be finding out about alternative sources of energy to see whether they'd be practical and economic. And so you know my experience last year finding out about wind power and solar power could be quite useful really.

Man: Yeah I should think it could. Do you think he was impressed?

Woman: I think he probably was actually. I mean he seemed quite impressed that I'd actually found out about the subjects before I'd come along to meet him and I knew what he was wanting to put over in his documentaries – um – and I think really by about half way through the meal he'd decided that he was going to give me the job, which was which was nice because I wasn't really expecting that, um... But then he went on and he started asking me all sorts of very very strange questions about my personal life, which I found very surprising.

Man: What sort of things?

Woman: Well he asked me whether I had a steady boyfriend, and er whether I was sort of – attached to anybody and er – and it was all a bit strange. I mean you hear about television producers wanting to know about your personal life, but I was...

Man: Why do you think he wanted to know all these things?

Woman: Well I think it must be because it's going to be a very demanding job and I'm going to have to travel quite a lot, and so obviously he wants to know whether I'm going to be free to do all of that.

Man: Mm you're quite sure it's not because he's interested in you himself?

Woman: Well, I really don't think so, but I mean I'll find out next week.

Man: Next week? What's happening next week?

Woman: Oh didn't I tell you? That's when I start the job.

Answers: (1) (a) Making TV documentaries; interviewed by the producer of the programmes.

(b) Very – she was offered the job.

(2) It took place over lunch; the interviewer told her she'd got the job half way through the interview; he asked her questions about her personal life.

(3) Any three of: what she'd done before; the jobs she'd had before; whether she'd got a degree; about her qualifications; whether she'd be interested in doing research for the documentaries.

(4) (a) She'd done her own research into energy.
    (b) She'd been to a centre for alternative technology and found out about different sources of energy.
    (c) The documentaries would also be about energy sources.

(5) Oil, coal, nuclear energy, and alternative energy sources, including wind power and solar power.

(6) Because she'd found out about the subject of the documentaries beforehand.

(7) (a) Whether she had a steady boyfriend; whether she was attached to anybody.
    (b) That he was interested in her himself; that he wanted to know if she would be free to do the job properly.

(8) Start the job.

Free practice

1 Divide the class into pairs. Students in each pair are either *both* A or *both* B. Working together, they prepare what they will say.
2 Students form new pairs, so that each pair has one A and one B. They act out the conversation.

Activities (following Unit 9)

PHOTOGRAPHS

> **Language:** This activity draws on language from:
> Unit 2 (Appearance)
> Unit 4 (Attitudes and reactions)
> Unit 7 (Deductions)
> Unit 9 (Clarifying)
> and also Intermediate units concerned with
> Description. (See Table 1 on p.3.)

This activity is a 'mock' oral examination. As in the Cambridge FCE Examination, students first describe the photograph, then answer other questions connected with it, then talk about related topics.

1 Look at the first photograph, and ask the class questions about it, e.g.:
   i) What kind of place is this a photo of?
      What's happening in the picture?
      What else can you see in the picture?
      What time of day do you think it is? Why?
      Look at the sign hanging in the middle of the picture. What do you think it represents?
      Why do you think the children have chosen this place to play?
   ii) Do you have shopping precincts like this in your country?
      How are they different?
      Do people do much skating in your country?
   iii) *Related topics:* Shopping
      Skating/Exercise
      Play facilities for children in cities

2 In pairs, students take it in turn to be the 'examiner' and the 'candidate'. Point out that the 'candidate' should talk as much as possible, with the 'examiner' prompting him with a question only when necessary – and that it is best to avoid questions which can be answered satisfactorily with a straight 'Yes' or 'No'. If you like, suggest some related topics for the 'examiners' to ask about, e.g.:

Picture 2	*Picture 3*
Holidays / the seaside	Cars
Summer and winter	The countryside
Being lost	Protecting the environment

COMPOSITION

> **Language:** The compositions can be used as a written
> extension to Activity 1. They can be
> approached in any way the student wishes, so
> may involve almost any language, but are
> especially likely to draw on language from
> Unit 4 (Advantages and disadvantages).

The writing can be done in class or for homework.

SITUATIONS

> **Language:** The situations draw on language from Units 7, 8
> and 9.

For procedure, see Activities following Unit 3.

Unit 10   Wishes and regrets

This continues a series of units in the Intermediate Course concerned with taking, initiating and commenting on *action*. It deals with language for wishing for changes, imagining oneself differently, and expressing regret.

The unit falls into two sections, followed by a general Free Practice exercise and a Reading Comprehension. The first section is concerned with wishing things would change, expressing dissatisfaction with the way things are, and imagining things differently. It practises structures with *I wish* and *If only*, and conditional structures with *If* + Past tense. The second section is concerned with expressing regret and criticising oneself; it practises *I wish* / *If only* + Past Perfect tense, conditionals with *If* + Past Perfect tense, and structures with modal verbs.

Assumed knowledge

Before beginning this unit, students should be familiar with:

Conditional structures (Intermediate Unit 23, Upper-Intermediate Units 7, 8).

Modals and past infinitives (Intermediate Unit 23, Upper-Intermediate Unit 7).

10.1   I WISH & IF ONLY
Presentation of: I wish / If only + would/could and Past tense.
Practice

10.2   CONFLICTING WISHES
Practice of: I wish / If only + Past tense; If + Past tense.

10.3   FANTASIES
Free practice
Writing

10.4   REGRET
Presentation and practice of: I wish / If only + Past perfect tense; should(n't) have done; If + Past Perfect tense.

10.5   FEELING SORRY FOR YOURSELF
Practice

10.6   I WISH I'D KNOWN: READING GAME
Practice of: could/ needn't have done.

10.7   WISHES AND REGRETS
Free practice
Writing

10.8   CHILDREN'S WISHES
Reading

10.1 I WISH & IF ONLY

> **Language:** Use of *I wish* and *If only*, for wishing for
> changes and expressing dissatisfaction with
> your present situation:
> i)   *I wish / If only + would...*
> ii) *I wish / If only + I/we could...*
> iii) *I wish / If only + Past tense*

Presentation

1 Look at the picture and briefly discuss what the man's problem is.
   Play the remarks on the tape.
2 Use Question (1) to establish that *I wish* and *If only* mean the same, and are
   used for wishing for changes that are not likely to take place.
3 Use Question (2) to establish these differences between the structures:
   i)   *I wish / If only + would* is used about things *you want to happen*. You
        don't think they *will* happen – but you wish they *would*.
   ii) *I wish / If only + could* is used about things *you want to do yourself*.
        They are things you *can't* do – but you wish you *could*.
   iii) *I wish / If only + Past tense* is used to talk about what's wrong with
        your present situation. You don't like the way things *are*, and you wish
        they *were* different.
4 Students make sentences for each situation. Use this section to show how *I
   wish + would* and *I wish + could* are used about single events and actions;
   I wish + Past tense is used about continuing states and situations:
   e.g. (a) I wish it *wasn't raining*.
              If only it *would stop* raining.
              I wish I *could go out*.
         (b) If only I *had* some friends.
              I wish someone *would visit* me.
              If only I *could meet* some nice people.

Practice

1 Look at the pictures and establish what's going on in each.
2 Either ask students to make sentences round the class, or let them look at
   the pictures in groups and go through the answers afterwards.
   ► W10 Ex 1 ◄

10.2 CONFLICTING WISHES   Practice

> **Language:** Practice of: *I wish* + Past tense.
> Conditional structures with *If* + Past tense, for
> imagining your present situation differently.

1 ⌨ Play the example on the tape. Point out the connection between *I wish* and *If* structures – both use the Past tense for *imagining* things about the present.
2 Go through the exercise and ask students to give just the *I wish* structures for each item:
   e.g. (1) I wish I had a telephone; I wish I didn't have a telephone.
3 Students have conversations in pairs, adding reasons each time.
   ▶ W10 Ex 2 ◀

10.3 FANTASIES

> **Language:** Free practice of 'Second Conditional' structures for 'fantasising'.

Free practice ⌨

This exercise begins with a Listening Model. (See 'Dealing with listening' in Part 3.)

A: If I had just one day I would go back to New York. I'd go up the Empire State Building, and I would take the ferry to Coney Island, and I would go on the funfair, and I would have a hot-dog and French fries and a very large glass of Coca Cola; and finally I think I would probably go to a show, and get a very expensive ticket and sit in the best seat in the house – and then I would fly home.

B: Well, if I could go anywhere in the world, I think I'd, I'd go to to Tibet and I'd go to Lhasa and I'd sit in a tea-house in Lhasa and I'd just watch people for an hour and then I'd get on a bus, I mean if they have buses in Tibet, and I'd travel through as much of Tibet as I could in one day.

C: If I could spend a day doing anything I wanted to, I'd like to go to London. I'd like to go to London and I'd like to buy some wonderful expensive clothes in a really...high-class shop and then, in the evening, I'd like to go out to one of these really expensive candle-lit restaurants and then afterwards I'd stay at a really nice hotel, you know nothing too...classy like the Savoy but really nice, really expensive.

1 Play the tape. Students answer the questions. Point out that the speakers use *If + Past...would...* because they are *imagining* unreal situations.
2 Divide the class into groups. Students take it in turns to interview the others in their group.
3 As a round-up, ask individual students what they found out from the people they interviewed.

Writing

The writing can be done in class or for homework.
   ▶ W10 Ex 3 ◀

10.4 REGRET   Presentation and practice

> **Language:** Use of the verb *regret*.
> Structures used in expressing regret:
> i)   *I wish / If only* + Past Perfect tense
> ii) *I should (n't) have done*
> iii) *If* + Past Perfect...*would(n't) have done*.

1 Read the text, and present any new vocabulary (e.g. stock market, invest, savings, collapse, safe, loan, embezzlement).
2 Look at (1). Ask students what else James regrets doing / not doing.
   e.g. He regrets taking money from the safe.
   Note: 'Regret' can also be followed by the past gerund ('He regrets having taken...') with no change in meaning. In the exercise, James could himself say 'I regret...ing...' instead of 'I wish I hadn't...'; this would, however, only be appropriate to a formal style of speech.
3 Look at the examples in (2). Establish that:
   i)   *I wish + Past Perfect tense* is used for talking about things you regret *in the past*.
   ii) *I should(n't) + have done* is used for criticising your own past mistakes.
   iii) *If + Past Perfect ...would(n't) have done* is used for imagining the past differently.
4 Students make sentences based on the text:
   e.g. I wish I hadn't taken money from the safe.
      I shouldn't have taken money from the safe.
      If I hadn't taken money from the safe, I wouldn't have been arrested.

10.5 FEELING SORRY FOR YOURSELF   Practice

> **Language:** Practice of language introduced in 10.4.

1 Ask students to suggest as many sentences as they can for each situation:
   e.g. (1) I wish I hadn't stayed in the sun so long.
      I should have worn a hat.
      If only I'd put some suntan lotion on.
      I should never have tried to cross the desert on foot, etc.
2 ▣ Play the example on the tape.
3 Divide the class into pairs. Students have conversations in pairs, based on the situations in (1) – (7).
4 As a round-up, ask different students what reasons they gave.
▶ W10 Ex 4 ◀

10.6 I WISH I'D KNOWN: READING GAME   Practice

> **Language:** Use of *needn't have done* and *could have done*
> for talking about unnecessary actions in the
> past and missed opportunities.
> Practice of *I wish* + Past Perfect tense.
> Practice of Reported speech (see Unit 6).

1 Read the example and establish that:
   i) I could have gone by bus = I didn't go by bus because I didn't know it
                        was possible;
   ii) I needn't have walked home = I walked home because I thought I had
                        to; now I know that it was unnecessary.
   Point out how the structures are formed:

could needn't	+ past infinitive

   This Reading Game is played in the same way as the one in 8.6, except that
   each section is read once only, and both parts of the sentence must be
   changed.
2 Divide the class into groups, and give each student a letter: A, B or C.
3 After going through the examples, demonstrate the game by reading out
   Student A's first sentence, using *I wish*:
   'I wish I'd known the lecture had been cancelled:'
   Ask all Students B and C to find a suitable continuation, and to change it to
   include *could have* or *needn't have*:
   'I could have stayed at home.'
   Point out that each sentence has only *one* continuation.
4 Give a few minutes for students to read through their own section silently.
   Answer any vocabulary questions.
5 Students play the game.
6 When most groups have finished, go through the answers with the class.
   Answers: A: (1) (See above.)
             (2) I wish you'd told me they were on the telephone: I needn't have
                  gone all the way to their house.
             (3) If only I'd realised that book was in the library: I needn't have
                  bought a copy.
             (4) I wish someone had told me he was a vegetarian: I could have
                  made an omelette.
        B: (1) If only I'd realised it was so near: I needn't have brought the car.
             (2) I wish someone had told me food would be provided: I needn't
                  have brought my own.
             (3) I wish you'd told me you had some money: we could have got a
                  taxi.
             (4) If only you'd mentioned that your friends played tennis: we
                  could have had a game of doubles.
        C: (1) I wish I'd realised you were on your own: I would have come
                  round for a game of cards.

101

(2) I wish you'd said you had a typewriter: I needn't have hired one.
(3) If only I'd known it would be such an informal party: I needn't have got changed.
(4) If only you'd told me you'd lost your umbrella: I could have lent you mine.

▶ W10 Ex 5 ◀

10.7 WISHES AND REGRETS

> **Language:** Free practice of language introduced in this unit.

Free practice

1 Point out that 'occupation' includes 'student'.
2 Either divide the class into pairs, forming new pairs for the second interview, or let students wander freely round the class interviewing whom they like.

Writing

The writing can be done in class or for homework.

10.8 CHILDREN'S WISHES   Reading

For procedure see 'Dealing with reading' in Part 3.
Answers: (1) Sarah and Rachel (and possibly Alana, who is regretting hitting her head with the trick-stick).
(2) A kind of toy which children whirl around their heads. Obviously they can be dangerous.
(3) She's wearing a dress that she doesn't like.
(4) (a) 'nap' = a little sleep, 'catnap' = to sleep like a cat; 'dash' = to go quickly, to run.
    (b) 'boarding school' = a school where the students live in, away from home; 'convent' = a school for girls run by a Catholic religious order.
    (c) 'mane' = hair on the back of the neck of a horse or a lion; 'shaggy' = long, thick and untidy; 'coat' = hair or fur on an animal's back; 'sleek' = smooth and shiny; 'den' = place where a wild animal lives.
(5) (This is a discussion question.)
(6) This is a discussion question, but the ages are:
Anne-Marie, Ian : 7
Adam, Alana, Rachel : 8
Sarah : 10
Vincent, Marian, Liza : 11
(7) Marian: spelling of 'choose'
Adam: apostrophes
Vincent: one punctuation mistake; spelling of 'their'

Sarah: capital 'S' in September
Ian: spelling of 'etc.' = et cetera
Anne-Marie: separation of 'a' 'round'
Liza: punctuation; spelling of 'which'
Alana: punctuation
- *shouldn't* can be used instead of *would(n't)* after *I* and *we*. In more formal English *were* is used instead of *was* after *I wish...*

Note: A possible extension to the exercise would be for the students to write similar paragraphs themselves.

Activities (following Unit 10)

JUNG'S DREAM

> **Language:** This activity draws on language from:
> Unit 1 (Experience)
> Unit 2 (Appearance)
> Unit 3 (Relating past events)
> Unit 7 (Deductions and explanations)
> and also Intermediate units concerned with
> Narration and Explanation. (See Table 1 on
> p.3.)

Either use the text and questions as a basis for class discussion; or let students read the text and discuss the questions in groups, and ask one student from each group to report their conclusions afterwards.

COMPOSITION

> **Language:** The composition is an extension of the
> previous activity, and draws on the same
> language areas.

The writing can be done in class or for homework.

Unit 11   Events in sequence

This is one of a series of units concerned with *narration* of past events. It deals with language for talking about the sequence of past events.

The unit falls into three sections, followed by a general Free Practice exercise and a Listening Comprehension. The first section is concerned with narrating events in sequence, and practises structures with *When, After* and *As soon as*. The second section is concerned with saying whether events happened in the right or wrong order, and practises structures with *(not) before* and *not...until*. The third section is concerned with unexpected past events, and practises structures with *had only just... when* and *no sooner had...than...*

Assumed knowledge

Before beginning this unit, students should be familiar with:
Use of Past and Past Perfect tenses for narration (Intermediate Units 15, 22, Upper-Intermediate Unit 3).
Past duration structures (Upper-Intermediate Unit 5).

11.1   WHEN...
Presentation and practice of: When + Past Simple; When/After + Past Perfect.

11.2   AS SOON AS
Practice of: As soon as + Past Simple and Past Perfect.

11.3   WHAT HAPPENED? READING GAME
Practice

11.4   GETTING THE ORDER RIGHT
Presentation and practice of: structures using 'before', 'not... before' and 'not...until'.

11.5   SUCCESS STORY
Free practice
Writing

11.6   UNEXPEC-TED EVENTS
Presentation and practice of: had only just... when...; no sooner had... than.... Practice

11.7   TELLING A STORY
Free practice
Writing

11.8   TWIN STORIES
Listening
Writing

11.1 WHEN... Presentation and practice

> **Language:** Two ways of connecting a series of events in
> the past:
> i) *When* + Past Simple
> ii) *When* $\Big|$ + Past Perfect.
>   *After*

1 Students join the events in the two stories.
  Establish that:
  i) The events in Story A must be joined using *When* + *Past Simple*:
     e.g. When Richard *opened* the cupboard, he saw a spider.
        When he *saw* the spider, he screamed.
     When + *Past Simple* is used to connect events that happen *almost at the same time*. It is especially used to describe a *reaction* to an event (e.g. opened – saw; saw – screamed).
  ii) The events in Story B must be joined using *When* + *Past Perfect*:
     e.g. When Richard's mother *had given* him his supper, she tucked him into bed.
        When she *had tucked* him into bed, she read him a story.
     When + *Past Perfect* is used to connect events that happen *one after the other* – one finishes before the other begins. *When* could be replaced by *After* here with no change in meaning.
2 Do the exercise round the class.

11.2 AS SOON AS Practice

> **Language:** Practice of *As soon as* + Past Simple and Past
> Perfect tenses.

1 Look at the example. Point out that *As soon as* can be used with either the Past Simple or the Past Perfect in the same way as *When*:
  i) *As soon as* + *Past Simple* is used for talking about an *immediate reaction* to something.
  ii) *As soon as* + *Past Perfect* is used to describe an event that took place *immediately after* another one.
2 Either do the exercise round the class or let students work through it in groups and go through the answers afterwards.

11.3 WHAT HAPPENED? READING GAME   Practice

> **Language:** Practice of language introduced in 11.1 and 11.2.

This Reading Game is played in the same way as the one in 8.6.
1 Divide the class into groups of three, and give each student a letter: A, B or C.
2 After going through the example, demonstrate the game by reading out Student A's sentence (1), changing it to:
   'When he took off his shoes and socks...'
Ask all Students B and C to look in their own section for a suitable continuation, and read it out:
   '...we all nearly suffocated from the smell'.
Then read out A's sentence (1) again, changing it to:
   'When he'd taken off his shoes and socks...'
Students B or C read out their other continuation:
   '...he got up and waded into the water'
3 Give a few minutes for students to read through their own section silently. Answer any vocabulary questions.
4 Students play the game.
5 When most groups have finished, go through the answers with the class.
   Answers: A: (1) (See above.)
              (2) When the doctor gave me an injection I felt a sharp pain in my arm.
                   When the doctor had given me an injection he wrote me a prescription.
              (3) As soon as I lit the gas there was a big explosion. When I'd lit the gas I put the kettle on.
          B: (1) When I opened the envelope I found a cheque for £5,000 inside.
                   When I'd opened the envelope I took out the letter and read it.
              (2) When he listened to the tape he got a splitting headache.
                   As soon as he'd listened to the tape he re-wound it and played it again.
              (3) When I paid the taxi driver I gave him a big tip. As soon as I'd paid the taxi driver I carried my suitcase into the hotel.
          C: (1) When I counted my change I realised they'd given me £5 too much.
                   When I'd counted my change I put it in my pocket.
              (2) When she kissed me I felt the earth move under my feet.
                   When she'd kissed me I went into the bathroom to wipe the lipstick off my face.
              (3) As soon as I got out of bed my legs gave way under me.
                   As soon as I'd got out of bed I got dressed.
Note: When and *As soon as* are alternatives throughout the exercise, although *As soon as* is obviously more natural for some items than others.
▶ W11 Ex 1 ◀

11.4 GETTING THE ORDER RIGHT

Presentation and practice

> **Language:** Describing past actions performed:
> i) in the correct (or expected) order:
>   He *did* X before he *did* Y
>   He *didn't do* Y until he*'d done* X
> ii) in the incorrect (or unexpected) order:
>   He *didn't do* X before he *did* Y
>   He *did* Y before he*'d done* X.

1 🔊 Play the examples on the tape and look at the picture. Point out that we use the Past Perfect tense when the second action in the sequence is mentioned before the first one:
   He didn't touch the wire until | he*'d* turn*ed* off the mains.
   He touched the wire before |
2 As a preparation for the groupwork, go through the exercise and establish which actions are in the right order, and which are in the wrong order.
3 In groups of three, students make sentences as in the examples.
4 The last part of the exercise is a free extension. Demonstrate it by telling the class about something you did in the wrong order.
5 In groups, students take it in turns to tell the others what they did.
   ▶ W11 Ex 2, Ex 3 ◀

11.5 SUCCESS STORY

> **Language:** Free practice of language introduced so far in this unit.

Free practice

1 Introduce the exercise by briefly discussing with the class some of the stages involved in each of the four 'enterprises'.
   Note: If any of your students have really started a successful enterprise of the same kind as those given (or knows someone who has), they should be encouraged to talk about that instead.
2 Divide the class into pairs. Each pair are either *both* A or *both* B. Working together, they prepare what they will say.
3 Students form new pairs, so that each pair has one A and one B. They interview each other and take brief notes.

Writing

The writing can be done in class or for homework.

11.6 UNEXPECTED EVENTS

> **Language:** Structures for talking about an *unexpected*
> event following immediately on another:
> i) *...had only just...when...*
> ii) *No sooner had...than...*

Presentation and practice

1 Present the structures by contrasting them with *As soon as*:
He finished his breakfast. Immediately after that he went out.

> As soon as he had finished his breakfast, he went out.
> (an expected, intended action)

He finished his breakfast. Then suddenly there was a knock on the door.

> He'd only just finished his breakfast when there was
> a knock on the door.
> No sooner had he finished his breakfast than there was
> a knock on the door.
> (an unexpected event)

Point out that:
  i) *had only just* and *no sooner had* are used with the same meaning, but
     the latter is appropriate to a more formal (especially written) style.
  ii) After *no sooner*, the subject and auxiliary must change places.
2 Look at the headline and the example.
3 Ask students to expand the other headlines; adding any details they think
  necessary.
  Possible answers: (1) The peace talks had only just got going when they broke down.
              (2) No sooner had the match started than one of the Manchester players
                  broke his leg.
              (3) The new king had only just begun his reign when he decided to
                  abdicate.
              (4) No sooner had the thief picked up the jewels than five policemen
                  came into the room and grabbed him.
              (5) No sooner had they started their honeymoon than the bride's first
                  husband appeared and demanded his wife back.
              (6) The casino had only just opened when a fire started and it was
                  destroyed.
              (7) The new tanker had only just set out on its maiden voyage when it
                  sank in a storm.

Practice

Either ask students to develop the sentences round the class or let them suggest
possible continuations in groups and go through the answers afterwards.
► W11 Ex 4 ◄

11.7 TELLING A STORY

> **Language:** Free practice of language introduced in this unit.
>
> *Note:* This exercise also draws on other 'narration' language introduced in Units 3 and 5 and also in Intermediate Units 12 and 22. (See Table 1 on p.3.) It would be a good idea to do some quick revision of this language, or at least remind students of it, before beginning the exercise.

Free practice

1 Read the beginning of the story, and point out how it expands the outline by filling in details of sequence, circumstances and previous events.
2 Look at the outline for the rest of the story and ask students to suggest ways of expanding it. (The notes are intentionally ambiguous, so the story could develop in various ways.)
3 Divide the class into groups. Either assign two stories to each group, or let them choose their own.
4 As a round-up, ask each group to tell one of their stories to the whole class.

Writing

The writing can be done in class or for homework.

11.8 TWIN STORIES

Listening 📼

In this Listening Comprehension there are two different, but related stories. The exercise is designed to be done as 'parallel listening'; that is, students divide into groups and listen to different stories, then tell each other the story they heard. If you do not have the equipment or space available, the exercise can be treated as a normal listening comprehension. (For procedure, see 'Dealing with listening' in Part 3.)
Here are two possible procedures for parallel listening:

In the classroom
1 Before the lesson, copy each story onto a different cassette, so that each group can listen to *one* of the two stories. (With large classes – 15 or more – you may need to have four groups, and to make two copies of each story.)
2 Divide the class into two (or four) groups, sitting as far away from each other as possible (ideally, in separate rooms). Give each group a cassette player and a cassette, and appoint one student to operate the machine. Each group listens to its own story, and answers the questions.
3 Students form pairs, so that each pair has one student from Group A and one student from Group B. In turn, they tell each other the story they heard.

4 Go through the questions with the whole class, asking the questions on Story 1 to students from Group B, and vice versa, to see how well they have retold their stories.

In the language laboratory

1 Before the lesson, record Story 1 onto half the student machines, and Story 2 onto the other half.

2 Students listen to the story on their machine and answer the questions. Make sure the same number of students are listening to each story!

3 and 4 Proceed as for Steps 3 and 4 above.

Note: The stories contain a few 'specialist' military words. Explain these before starting the exercise:

RAF = Royal Air Force = the 'flying' section of the armed forces.

National Service = period everyone has to spend in the army, navy or air force. (This no longer exists in Britain, but existed when the speaker was young.)

Khaki = greenish brown, the colour of army uniforms.

To be 'demobbed' = demobilised = released from military service.

Story 1

As soon as my twin brother and I reached the age of 18, we joined the RAF, the Royal Air Force, where we did our National Service for two years. Usually the Air Ministry allowed twins to stay together for their service but on this occasion we didn't. In fact soon after we'd joined I went overseas and did my service in Iraq, and Ken stayed in England.

Well, when we got to Iraq, we were all issued with RAF uniforms, which of course in a hot climate like the Middle East included khaki shorts. I thought it would be rather fun to send a photograph back so as soon as I got my uniform I went out and had a photograph taken of myself standing by a camel, and this photograph was then sent back to my brother. Now Ken worked in RAF photographic intelligence, and he was able in the Air Ministry dark rooms to make an enlargement of this ridiculous photo of me in my shorts with this camel. And unfortunately for Ken, the enlargement was seen by the squadron leader in charge of his section, and he accused him of using Air Ministry materials for his own private use, which of course was absolutely true. And then he said 'And anyway Binney, what on earth

are you doing standing beside a camel?' and Ken said 'It's not me sir – it's my twin brother' but of course the squadron leader wouldn't believe him – you see, we're absolutely exactly identical twins – and he was convinced that Ken had nipped off abroad secretly for a holiday or something, which of course was absolutely ridiculous, and the result was that poor brother Ken got 14 days confined to barracks.

Story 2

As soon as my twin brother and I reached the age of 18, we joined the RAF, the Royal Air Force, where we did our National Service for two years. Usually the Air Ministry allowed twins to stay together for their service but on this occasion we didn't. In fact soon after we'd joined I went overseas and did my service in Iraq, and Ken stayed in England.

Well, we'd done our two years' national service, he in England and me in Iraq, and the time approached when we were both going to be demobbed. So before I left Iraq I did a lot of sunbathing and got a really super tan. So I travelled 3500 miles back to the UK and as soon as I had been released from the RAF I packed my bags and got a train down from

London to my home town. The train arrived at about six o'clock in the evening so there I was in the south of England in a rather cold March with this magnificent suntan. Anyway I'd only just left the station when a taxi drew up and I got in. And no sooner had I sat down and given the address than the most amazing thing happened, because the taxi driver looked at me and he said to me in a wonderful Cockney accent 'Cor. I've only just taken you 'ome already'. I said 'Well I'm sorry, you couldn't have done that because I've only just come back from Iraq'. He said 'No – I took you 'ome already', he said, 'You was with an elderly gentleman and you were going to the same address. But – 'ow did you get so brown?' Of course, immediately he said that I realised that his previous fare had been my brother, who'd been released on the same day, and that my father had been at the station to meet him. And this was confirmed when we arrived at my house and there was my pale twin brother coming out of the door to welcome me home.

Answers: *Group A*
(1) While he was doing his National Service in the RAF.
(2) (a) In Iraq.
    (b) In England.
(3) They were identical twins.
(4) (a) To show what he looked like in his uniform.
    (b) Speaker wearing RAF uniform with khaki shorts, standing by a camel in the desert.
(5) He enlarged it; he worked in RAF photographic intelligence, and could use the Air Ministry dark rooms.
(6) (a) Using Air Ministry materials for his own private use; going for a secret holiday abroad.
    (b) He couldn't possibly have gone abroad secretly.
(7) Fourteen days confined to barracks (= he couldn't leave the barracks).

Group B
(1) When he was demobilised.
(2) (a) Iraq. (b) England.
(3) They were identical twins.
(4) Went sunbathing, left Iraq, arrived in England, left the RAF, got a train to his home town, got in a taxi, arrived home.
(5) His twin brother and his father.
(6) (a) In Iraq.
    (b) Because his brother looked exactly the same, but had no suntan. The taxi driver thought they were the same person, and couldn't understand where the suntan had come from.

Writing

The writing can be done in class or for homework.

Activities (following Unit 11)

LIFE-STYLES

> **Language:** This activity draws on language from:
> Unit 4 (Attitudes and reactions)
> Unit 8 (Advantages and disadvantages)
> Unit 10 (Wishes and regrets)
> and also Intermediate units concerned with
> Personal information and Comparison. (See
> Table 1 on p.3.)

1 Introduce the activity by discussing what other characteristics the life-styles of the two people might have.
2 Divide the class into pairs. Students in each pair are either *both* A or *both* B. Working together, they prepare what they will say.
3 Students form new pairs, so that each pair has one A and one B. They act out the conversation.

COMPOSITION

> **Language:** The compositions can be approached in any
> way the student wishes (e.g. an abstract
> discussion of the topic, an anecdote, an
> account of himself) and may involve any
> language.

The writing can be done in class or for homework.

Unit 12   Comparison

This is one of a series of units concerned with *comparison* and evaluation. It deals with language for talking about large and small differences, making precise comparisons and comparisons involving different times.

The unit falls into three sections, followed by a Reading Comprehension. The first section is concerned with talking about large and small differences, and practises the use of 'degree' adverbs in comparison structures. The second section is concerned with making precise comparisons and practises numerical comparison structures. The third section is concerned with comparisons involving different times, and practises structures using different tenses and modal verbs.

Assumed knowledge

Before beginning this unit, students should be familiar with:
Basic comparison of adjectives and adverbs (Intermediate Unit 9).
Structures for comparing the past and the present (Intermediate Unit 10).
Structures for talking about similarities and differences (Intermediate Unit 17).

12.1 LARGE AND SMALL DIFFERENCES

> **Language:** Degree adverbs in comparisons to show how
> large or small a difference is:
> e.g. *much / a lot / far more...than...*
> *a little / a bit / slightly more...than...*
> *almost / nearly as...as...*
> *not quite / not nearly as...as...*
> Comparison of adjectives and adverbs
> (revision).

Presentation and practice

1 Read the two reports. Introduce any new vocabulary (e.g. *brand new, an old hand, to socialise*).
2 Look at the examples, and discuss (1). Build up these tables on the board to show the range of adverbs that can be used:

Big difference

Paradise Holidays are	much a lot far considerably	more expensive than Vista Tours.

Small difference

Paradise Holidays are	a little a bit slightly	longer than Vista Tours.

3 Ask students to make other comparisons between the tours, based on the notes:
   e.g. The coaches on Vista Tours are a bit older than those on Paradise Tours, but they're cleaner.
4 Look at the examples of *(not)...as...as* structures.
   Establish that:
   i)   *not nearly as* expensive *as* = much cheaper than
   ii) *almost / nearly / not quite as* long *as* = a little shorter than.
5 Students make comparisons between the tours using *(not)...as...as...* structures. For variety, this stage could be done in groups.

Writing

The writing can be done in class or for homework.
▶ **W12 Ex 1** ◀

12.2 SIMILARITIES AND DIFFERENCES   Free practice

> **Language:** Free practice of language introduced in 12.1.

1 Demonstrate the pairwork by choosing one student and comparing your physical appearance and dress with his. Ask the rest of the class to make comments.
2 Working in pairs, students compare themselves with their partner.
3 Students form new pairs (this can be easily done by each student turning round to face the person on his other side). They tell their new partners what they found out.

12.3 COMPARING PRICES   Presentation and practice

> **Language:** Numerical comparison structures for comparing prices.

1 Ask students to complete the three sentences, and present the structures by writing this table on the board:

Steak is about three times	as expensive as the price of	chicken.
Steak costs about three times as much as chicken.		
Chicken is about a third	as expensive as the price of	steak.

Point out that with twice, three times, four times, etc., we use *as...as...* or *the (noun) of...*; we don't usually say 'three times more expensive than...'.
2 Ask students to compare the other items in the same way:
  e.g. Frozen peas are nearly twice as expensive as tinned peas.
       Tinned peas are almost half the price of frozen peas.
3 ▣ Play the example on the tape.
4 Students have similar conversations about the other items.

12.4 MEASURING OTHER DIFFERENCES   Practice

> **Language:** Practice of numerical comparisons using:
> as + adjective + as
> the + noun + of
> 'Dimension' nouns: height, depth, length, width, thickness, weight, speed.

1 Build up the list of nouns on the board, asking students to tell you what they are and also to spell them.

2 Point out that the adjectives and nouns in the table can be used with the same structures as the prices in 12.3:

e.g. Everest is nearly | twice as high as / twice the height of | Mont Blanc.

3 Students look at the pictures and make as many comparisons as they can about the pictures, using the words in the table.

► W12 Ex 2 ◄

12.5 WHAT IS IT?   Free practice 🔊

> **Language:** Free practice of language introduced so far in this unit.

This exercise begins with a Listening Model. (See 'Dealing with listening' in Part 3.)

A: Right, um, it's made of pottery.

B: Pottery, mm. Is this object bigger or smaller than a refrigerator?

A: Oh, much smaller.

B: I see. How big is it compared to a flower pot?

A: Um – it's a bit smaller than a flower pot.

C: Does it have a similar shape to a packet of cigarettes?

A: No, it doesn't.

C: What about a flower pot? Is it the same shape as a flower pot?

A: Yes, it's about the same shape as a flower pot.

B: Would I use it more often than I'd use a flower pot?

A: Oh yes, much more often.

B: More often than a packet of cigarettes?

A: Well that depends on how much you smoke.

C: Might I use it at the same time as I use a packet of cigarettes?

A: You might do, yes.

B: Is it a coffee cup?

A: Yes, it is.

1 Play the tape. Stop the tape before the end and ask students to tell you what the object is and also how the game is played.

2 Play the tape again. Students answer Question (2):

e.g. It's a completely different shape from a postcard.
    It's much smaller than a refrigerator.

3 Elicit from the class the different questions that were asked, referring to:
   (a) a refrigerator
   (b) a flower pot
   (c) a packet of cigarettes
   If necessary, write these structures on the board:

> How (big) is it compared to...?
> Is it the same (size) as...?
> Does it have a similar (shape) to...?

4 Point out that in the game, students can ask two kinds of question:
   i) 'Comparison' questions:
      e.g. Is it bigger or smaller than a refrigerator?

117

ii) 'Similarity' questions:
    e.g. Is it the same shape as a flower pot?
Demonstrate the game by thinking of an object yourself, saying what it's made of, and asking the class to guess what it is.
4 Students play the game in groups, taking it in turns to think of an object.
5 A possible extension to this activity is for each group to choose one of the objects they guessed and to try it out on the rest of the class.

12.6 COMPARISONS WITH DIFFERENT TENSES   Presentation and practice

> **Language:** Comparisons involving different tenses and different verbs.

1 Look at the examples. Focus students' attention on them by asking them to 're-construct' what each one means:
    e.g. Yesterday it was quite warm, but today it isn't.
        The weather forecast said it would be warm, but it isn't.
2 Point out that the examples show three types of comparison:
  i)   Comparisons involving different tenses of the same verb:
      e.g. They *gave* us less food than they usually *do*.
  ii) Comparisons involving modals:
      e.g. They *gave* us less food than they *should have done*.
 iii) Comparisons between reality and what was expected:
      e.g. They *gave* us less food than they*'d said* they would.
If you like, give more examples of your own of each type.
3 Establish that:
  i)   The verb *be* is always repeated in the second part of the comparison. Build up these examples on the board, by giving situations (e.g. 'Last year the weather was bad, this year it's good') and asking students to give comparison structures:

The weather <u>was</u> worse last year than	it <u>is</u> this year it should have <u>been</u> you said it would <u>be</u> I'd expected it to <u>be</u>

  ii) Other verbs are replaced by a form of *do* or (if infinitives) omitted. Build up these examples on the board in the same way:

He <u>didn't work</u> as hard last year as	he <u>does</u> now he should <u>have done</u> you'd said he would I'd expected him to

4 Look at sentence openings (1) – (4). Ask students to suggest as many continuations as possible for each.

5 Either do the exercise with the whole class, or let students do it in groups and go through the answers afterwards.
► W12 Ex 3, Ex 4 ◄

12.7 NOT WHAT I'D EXPECTED

> **Language:** Free practice of language introduced in 12.6.
>
> *Note:* This exercise concentrates on comparisons between reality and what was expected.

Free practice

1 🔊 Play the text on the tape. Check general comprehension by asking questions:
  e.g. In what ways did the speaker like her new job?
  In what ways didn't she like it?
  Why do you think it was satisfying?
2 Demonstrate the groupwork by telling the class about a place you visited that was different from what you'd expected.
3 Divide the class into groups for the activity. Either assign one topic to each member of the group, or let them choose their own.
4 As a possible round-up, ask each group to tell their most interesting story to the rest of the class.

Writing

The writing can be done in class or for homework.

12.8 DIETING REVOLUTION

Reading

For procedure, see 'Dealing with reading' in Part 3.
Answers: (1) They gain weight by eating and drinking more calories than they use up in energy; they lose weight by eating fewer calories than they use up in energy.
  (2) They are much higher in calories.
  (3) Fats that you can't see (e.g. in protein foods). They mean the food has far more calories than people imagine.
  (4) (a) Because it seems as though the slimmer is really eating very little.
  (b) Because it's very high in calories.
  (5) (a) Butter has more than twice as many calories as flour.
  (b) Tongue has about twice as many calories as chicken.
  (c) Flour has slightly fewer calories than sugar.
  (d) Cheddar cheese has nearly three times as many calories as chicken.

     (e) Mushrooms have far fewer calories than margarine (about a fiftieth of the number).

(6) The low-fat slimmer eats far more food (in quantity), but consumes far fewer calories.

(7) It allows you to eat a lot of food, only make small changes in your eating habits, but still greatly reduce the number of calories you consume.

Discussion

Either use the questions as a basis for discussion with the whole class, or let students discuss them in groups and report their conclusions to the rest of the class afterwards.

Writing

The writing can be done in class or for homework.

Activities (following Unit 12)

QUIZ

This quiz is designed for two teams of four students, with the rest of the class acting as an audience. Other possibilities are just to ask the questions around the class, or to divide the class into four (or eight) groups competing with each other.

Suggested procedure
1 Divide the class in groups or teams.
2 At the beginning of each round, explain how it works, and give the example where appropriate.
3 Ask each of the team members one question each. Give two points for a correct answer. If the answer is wrong, offer the question to the opposing team for one point.

Eight different rounds of questions are given below. Some rounds relate directly to the course, some are more general. They can be used as they stand, or a selection could be made – and supplemented with your own rounds of suitable questions. Answers are given in bold type.

Round 1: Double meanings

In this round, contestants are given two definitions and asked to find a word which means both.

Example: Not heavy – not dark
Answer: **light**

1 Part of an examination – writing material	**paper**
2 Reserve a place – reading material	**book**
3 Keep an eye on – something you wear	**watch**
4 Part of the hand – something you hit	**nail**
5 Container – to fight with gloves on	**box**
6 Room – where astronauts go	**space**
7 Type or sort – nice to other people	**kind**
8 Circle of metal – use the phone	**ring**

Round 2: Meanings into words

Contestants are asked questions about 'facts' in the units so far.

1 What title did Lucy give to the Magritte painting in Unit 2?
A stony home.

2 What was Mr Wilkinson's last injury, and how was it caused?
He broke his leg. He fell off the stretcher and fell downstairs.
3 What topic was discussed in the radio programme 'Opinions' in Unit 4?
Television commercials / advertising.
4 What sign of the Zodiac was the writer in the astrology passage?
Gemini.
5 What was Mr Lock's problem?
He bought an electric drill that didn't work.
6 What happened to Dr Griffiths on 2 April 1983?
An ice-block fell out of the sky and landed near him.
7 How did the Government of Tango solve its economic problems?
They exported the drug.
8 What crime did James commit in the unit about wishes and regrets?
Embezzlement.

Round 3: They sound the same

In this round, contestants are given definitions of two words which sound the
same (but are spelled differently), and asked to name the two words.

Example: A number – didn't lose
Answer: **one/won**

1 Kind of fruit – two together	**pear/pair**
2 Short rest (e.g. between lessons) – the middle pedal in a car	**break/brake**
3 Took hold of – where people are put on trial	**caught/court**
4 Certain – where the land meets the water	**sure/shore**
5 Not as near – parent	**farther/father**
6 Something you dig – complete	**hole/whole**
7 Change colour – stop breathing	**dye/die**
8 Rain heavily – not having much money	**pour/poor**

Round 4: Verbs

Contestants are given a definition of a verb and asked to name it. The first
letter of the answer is given as a clue.

Example: To make you very frightened (T)
Answer: **terrify**

1 To annoy (I)	**irritate**
2 To give a nasty surprise to (S)	**shock**
3 To say someone has committed a crime (A)	**accuse**
4 To promise to do something nasty to someone (T)	**threaten**
5 To offer someone money to do something (often illegally) (B)	**bribe**
6 To make it possible for someone to do something (E)	**enable**
7 To make someone do something (F)	**force**
8 To do up a seat-belt, for example (F)	**fasten**

Round 5: Anagrams

In this round contestants are given a very loose definition and an anagram of the answer to help them find it.

Example: Something to eat you can get from *beard*
Answer: **bread**

1 A place in the open you can get from *danger*	**garden**
2 A time you can get from *thing*	**night**
3 An animal you can get from *shore*	**horse**
4 Part of the body you can get from *earth*	**heart**
5 Part of a desk you can get from *reward*	**drawer**
6 A reporting verb you can get from *eager*	**agree**
7 Something on the wall you can get from *flesh*	**shelf**
8 A musician you can get from *resign*	**singer**

Round 6: Comparisons

This round will involve a lot of guesswork: ask *each* contestant for an answer, and then give the point to the nearest guess.

1 How big (in volume) is the Earth compared with the Moon?
   About 50 times as big.
2 How much heavier is a kilo than a pound?
   A bit more than twice as heavy.
3 How much longer is a metre than a foot?
   A bit more than three times as long.
4 How many sheep are there in Australia compared with the number of people?
   About 12 times as many sheep as people.
5 How much faster can a cheetah run than a man?
   Almost three times as fast.
6 John drives 40 kilometres. Jill drives 25 miles. Who drives further, and by how much?
   They both drive the same distance.

Round 7: Word building

Contestants are given a 'base' word and a definition of another word. They are asked to build on the base word to produce the answer.

Example: Add something to the word *name* to make a word meaning 'family name'.
Answer: **surname**

1 Add something to the word *ordinary* to make a word meaning 'strange', 'very unusual'.	**extraordinary**
2 Add something to the word *event* to make a word meaning 'at last'.	**eventually**

3 Add something to the word *appoint* to make a word
   meaning 'not as good as you expected'.   disappointing
4 Add something to the word *trust* to make a word
   meaning 'honest', 'reliable'.   trustworthy
5 Add something to the word *comment* to make a person
   who comments on a sporting event on TV.   commentator
6 Add something to the word *understand* to make a word
   meaning 'to fail to understand properly'.   misunderstand
7 Add something to the word *courage* to make a word
   meaning 'to stop someone wanting to do something'.   discourage
8 Add something to the word *corrupt* to make a word
   meaning 'not capable of being bribed'.   incorruptible

Round 8: About Britain

This round could be included with classes in British language schools, or if
students are likely to have visited Britain.

1 What is the capital of Scotland?   Edinburgh
2 What is the capital of Wales?   Cardiff
3 What town is associated with Shakespeare?   Stratford-on-Avon
4 Where in London can you find Eros?   Piccadilly Circus
5 Where is King's College Chapel?   Cambridge
6 What is the Queen's address?   Buckingham Palace
7 What is the Prime Minister's address?   10 Downing Street
8 What is the population of London (to the nearest million)?   10 million

COMPOSITION

Language:	The compositions draw on language from the following units:
	Compositions (1) and (2): Unit 4 (Attitudes and reactions)
	Unit 7 (Deductions and explanations)
Composition (3):	Unit 3 (Relating past events)
	Unit 6 (Reporting)
	Unit 11 (Events in sequence)

The writing can be done in class or for homework.

SITUATIONS

Language: The situations draw on language from Units 10, 11 and 12.

For procedure, see Activities following Unit 3.

Unit 13   Processes

This is one of a series of units concerned with *explanation* and speculation about the past, present and future. It deals with language for describing the stages of a process, giving instructions, and explaining how things work.

The unit falls into two sections, followed by a Listening Comprehension. The first section is concerned with the sequence of stages in a process; it practises the 'sequence' structures introduced in Unit 11, but used here for talking 'in general'. The second section is concerned with describing natural processes and explaining how things work; it introduces a range of 'change of state' verbs, and practises the Passive.

Assumed knowledge

Before beginning this unit, students should be familiar with:
Present Simple Passive and Present Perfect Passive (Intermediate Units 3, 10).
'Effect' verbs (Upper-Intermediate Unit 8).
Sequence structures (Upper-Intermediate Unit 11).

13.1 WHEN...
Presentation and practice of: When + Present Simple and Present Perfect. Practice

13.2 EMPHASISING THE RIGHT ORDER
Practice of: before; not ...before/until.

13.3 GIVING INSTRUCTIONS
Free practice
Writing

13.4 NATURAL PROCESSES
Presentation and practice of: 'change of state' verbs.

13.5 SCIENCE FOR EVERYONE
Practice

13.6 THE PASSIVE IN DESCRIBING PROCESSES
Practice of: Passive structures.

13.7 HOW THINGS WORK
Free practice
Writing

13.8 MAKING YOUR OWN WINE
Listening
Writing

13.1 WHEN...

> **Language:** Two kinds of sequence connected with *When...*
> i) *When* + Present Simple
> ii) *When* + Present Perfect.
>
> *Note:* The distinction between the two types is the same as
> that introduced in 11.1, but applied to the *present* for
> describing processes and giving instructions.

Presentation and practice

1 Read the two sets of sentences, and discuss the difference between them.
From students' answers, establish that:
   i) *When + Present Simple* is used to connect two events that happen almost
   at the same time. It is especially used to describe a *reaction* to an event.
   ii) *When + Present Perfect* is used to connect two events that happen one
   after the other. It is especially used in giving a series of instructions. In
   this type of sequence, *When* can be replaced by *after* or *after that*:
   e.g. When | you*'ve cut* off the cheese, you place it in the trap.
         After |
   First you cut off the cheese. *After that* you place it in the trap.
2 Ask students to construct pairs of sentences based on the prompts:
   e.g. When you arrive at the border, you have to show your passport.
         When you've shown your passport, you go to the Customs.
   Note: For the first sentence in each pair, students must choose between
   When + Present Simple or *When + Present Perfect*; the second sentence in
   the pair will use *When + Present Perfect* in every case.

Practice

1 Introduce any necessary vocabulary: e.g. (b) receiver, dial, slot, dialling
tone, ringing tone; (c) inner tube, patch, pump.
2 In groups, students discuss each of the processes.
3 Go through each process with the class.

13.2 EMPHASISING THE RIGHT ORDER   Practice

> **Language:** Use of *before* and *not before / not until* to
> emphasise a correct sequence:
> You should do X *before* you *do* Y
> You shouldn't do Y | *before* | you*'ve done* X
> | *until* |
>
> *Note:* These structures are similar to those introduced in
> 11.4.

1 ☷ Play the example on the tape, and point out the relationship between these structures and those in 11.4.
2 Demonstrate the groupwork by doing (1) with the whole class.
3 Students do the exercise in groups of three, taking it in turns to begin.
4 Go through the exercise with the class.
▶ **W13 Ex 1** ◀

13.3   GIVING INSTRUCTIONS

Free practice ☷

> **Language:** Free practice of language introduced so far in this unit.

This exercise begins with a Listening Model. (See 'Dealing with listening' in Part 3.)

A: How do you make Turkish coffee? What is it you have to do exactly?
B: Well, say you want to make four cups of coffee. O.K? You put four cups of cold water, and four level teaspoons of sugar in the coffee pot. Then you light the gas, and put the coffee on the stove. Now when the water boils, you take the coffee pot off the stove and pour a bit of the water into one of the cups. Then you put the four heaped teaspoons of coffee in the coffee pot, and stir it. Now it's very important not to put the coffee in before you've poured some water off, or else it'll overflow and make a terrible mess. So anyway, you put the pot back on the stove and let the coffee come back to the boil very slowly. When it starts to boil, the coffee will rise slowly up to the top of the pot, and when it reaches the top, you take it off the stove. O.K? Before you pour the coffee out, you should pour back the water that you poured off earlier. Remember? – and this helps to make the grounds settle. See? O.K?
A: Yes, thanks very much.

1 Play the tape. Students answer Question (1).
   Answer: Turkish coffee.
2 Play the tape again. Students make notes in the columns provided.
3 Ask students to give the instructions they heard, using their notes.
4 Discuss with the class how they would make coffee themselves. If you like, ask students to actually give *instructions* for making coffee by their own method.
5 Give a few minutes for students to think of a process they know about and prepare to give instructions (either let students choose their own topics, or use the ones in the pictures).
6 Divide the class into groups. In turn, they give instructions to the others in their group. The others take brief notes.

Writing

The writing can be done in class or for homework.
► W13 Ex 2 ◄

13.4 NATURAL PROCESSES   Presentation and practice

Language: Intransitive verbs for describing changes of state.

1 Ask students to match the verbs with the five categories, and make sure they understand what they mean.
Answers: (1) *Changes in size*: expand, contract, shrink, stretch, swell.
(2) *Solids becoming liquid*: melt, dissolve.
(3) *Liquids becoming solid*: set, freeze, congeal.
(4) *Liquids becoming gas*: evaporate.
(5) *Gases becoming liquid*: condense.
2 Either go through the questions with the whole class, or let them discuss them in groups and go through the answers afterwards.
► W13 Ex 4 ◄

13.5 SCIENCE FOR EVERYONE   Practice

Language: Practice of language introduced in 13.4. *When* + Present Simple for describing natural reactions.

1 Divide the class into groups to discuss the problems.
2 Discuss the answers with the whole class:
Answers (1) Alcohol freezes at a lower temperature than water, so when it comes into contact with the ice in the lock, it melts it.
(2) When you pour boiling water into a glass, it heats the inside surface, which then expands. The outside of the glass heats and expands more slowly – this makes the glass crack.
(3) Water evaporates when the sun shines on it, and forms water vapour. The water vapour rises, and as it rises it cools. As it cools, it condenses to form clouds. If the clouds cool even more (e.g. when they cross high ground), they will condense further and fall as rain.
(4) The air in the car cools down, and the water vapour condenses on the coldest surfaces, i.e. the windows (not on the seats because they remain as warm as the air inside the car).
(5) Pipes only burst if they have water in them. When the temperature drops below zero, the water freezes and expands as it turns to ice. This makes the pipes burst.

13.6 THE PASSIVE IN DESCRIBING PROCESSES   Practice

> **Language:** Use of the passive in describing processes, when the agent is unimportant, unknown or self-evident.
> Further practice of *When* + Present Simple and Present Perfect tenses.

1 Look at the pictures with the class, and ask students to give a *coherent* description of the stages involved, paying special attention to sentence connectives.
2 Divide the class into groups to discuss the other three processes. Point out that students are *not* expected to know what all the stages are. They should talk about those they know, and try to imagine what the other stages might be.
Discuss the answers with the whole class.
▶ W13 Ex 3, Ex 5 ◀

13.7 HOW THINGS WORK

> **Language:** Free practice of language introduced in this unit.
> Practice of 'effect' verbs: *allow, make, enable, prevent,* etc. (see 8.1).

Free practice

1 Read the text, and point out the use of 'effect' verbs.
2 Either look at the other diagrams with the whole class, or divide the class into groups and let each group work out a description of one of the processes and then report back to the rest of the class.

Writing

The writing can be done in class or for homework.

13.8 MAKING YOUR OWN WINE

Listening 📼

This is a Listening Comprehension Passage. For procedure, see 'Dealing with listening' in Part 3.

Interviewer: Is it very difficult to make your own wine?

Man: No I wouldn't say it was difficult at all. The one thing you've got to remember when making your own wine is to keep everything spotlessly clean. Other than that it's really just a question of following very basic instructions.

Interviewer: Now supposing I want to make a gallon of wine. What do I need?

Man: Well, you'll need some water and some sugar, which are both fairly easy to obtain, and also of course you'll need some grape juice, which nowadays you can buy in tins in one of the many wine shops that there are. Other than that you'll need some yeast and a few pieces of basic equipment.

Interviewer: O.K. So I've got my ingredients and my equipment. What do I do now?

Man: Well you want to make a gallon of wine. The first thing you do is you take a large glass jar which we call a demijohn. Into this jar you put your grape juice, you top it up with warm water, add your sugar and finally you put in your yeast, and you seal off the whole jar with an airlock. Then you put the jar in a warm place and then you just leave it for two or three weeks to ferment.

Interviewer: It's the yeast that makes the wine ferment, isn't it?

Man: Yes, that's right. Fermentation just means the production of alcohol. What happens is that the yeast inside the jar feeds on the sugar and multiplies. Now as it does this it converts the sugar into two parts — one part is alcohol, which of course the wine maker is interested in, and the other part is carbon dioxide, which of course is not needed.

Interviewer: And so what do you do then?

Man: Well, you put some chemicals into the jar which will prevent the fermentation starting again later when you don't want it to, and then you find a nice cool place and you leave the jar there for about a week. The reason for this is the wine is full of dead yeast cells and other things that you don't want in the finished product, and over the week these will settle at the bottom. Now after these things have all settled at the bottom you want to separate the wine from all this rubbish and so you get a long plastic tube and you syphon the wine off the rubbish into another clean jar.

Interviewer: I see. So when you've syphoned it how long do you have to wait before you can drink it after that?

Man: Oh I think this depends on the type of wine that you're making. Some makes you can drink almost immediately and they taste fairly good. Others you're supposed to leave for six or twelve months before you drink them.

Interviewer: It sounds as though it's quite a lot of work. Is it really worth it?

Man: Oh financially it's very much worth while. I think you can make home-made wine at about a quarter or a fifth of the price that it would cost you to buy wine in the shops. And quite apart from that you get a wonderful sense of satisfaction when you produce a bottle of wine at a dinner party, say, and you can say that I made this myself.

Interviewer: So it's cheap, then, but is it

as good as the wine you buy in the shops?

Man: Yes, well, I thought you'd ask me that. I think the best way to answer that question would be for you to try it yourself. I happen to have a bottle with me so...

Interviewer: Thank you very much.

Man: O.K?

Interviewer: Mm. That's very good.

Answers: PART 1

(1) Keep everything spotlessly clean.
(2) Water, sugar, grape juice, yeast.
(3) Seal the jar with an airlock.
    Put the jar in a warm place.

PART 2

(4) The production of alcohol.
(5) It feeds on the sugar and converts it into alcohol and carbon dioxide.

PART 3

(6) (a) To prevent the fermentation starting again.
    (b) To allow the dead yeast to settle.
(7) (a) It's syphoned through a long plastic tube.
    (b) So that you don't disturb the sediment.
(8) It depends on the type of wine: immediately – 12 months.

PART 4

(9) It's much cheaper than shop wine.
    It gives you a sense of satisfaction.
(10) The interviewer tries some home-made wine.

Writing

The writing can be done in class or for homework.

Activities (following Unit 13)

LANGUAGE SCHOOL

Language: This activity draws on language from:
Unit 5 (Duration)
Unit 8 (Advantages and disadvantages)
Unit 9 (Clarifying)
Unit 12 (Comparison)
and also Intermediate units concerned with
Personal information and Comparison. (See
Table 1 on p.3.)

1 Choose four students to be 'students'. Divide the rest of the class into four groups, each group representing one of the language schools. The 'students' prepare individually, the language school representatives prepare in their groups.
2 Each of the 'students' visits each language school in turn to have an interview.
3 As a round-up, ask each 'student' to say which language school he has chosen and why.

COMPOSITION

Language: The compositions allow for a wide range of language, but draw on most of the same language areas as the previous activity.

The writing can be done in class or for homework.

Unit 14 Prediction

This is one of a series of units concerned with *explanation* and speculation about the past, present and future. It deals with language for predicting future actions and events, expressing probability in predictions, and predicting the consequences of future events.

The unit falls into three sections, followed by a Reading Comprehension and a general Free Practice exercise. The first section is concerned with saying how likely or unlikely things are to happen, and practises a range of appropriate prediction structures. The second section is concerned with making conditional predictions, and practises structures with *If, Unless, As long as,* and *Provided that.* The third section is concerned with predicting and imagining the consequences of future events, and contrasts conditional structures with *will* and *would.*

Assumed knowledge

Before beginning this unit, students should be familiar with:

Basic prediction structures using adverbs and modals (Intermediate Unit 19).

Use of Future Simple, Future Continuous and Future Perfect tenses in making predictions (Intermediate Unit 19).

Use of conditional structures with 'would' for imagining consequences (Intermediate Unit 23, Upper-Intermediate Units 8, 10).

14.1 DEGREES OF PROBABILITY
Presentation and practice of: bound to / sure to / certain to; likely to, unlikely to. Practice

14.2 PRE-CAUTIONS
Practice

14.3 HORO-SCOPES
Writing

14.4 CON-DITIONAL PREDICTIONS
Presentation and practice of: If, Unless, As long as, Provided (that) + Present Simple.

14.5 IN YOUR LIFETIME
Free practice
Writing

14.6 PREDICTING CONSEQUENCES
Presentation of:
If + Present... will...; If + Past... would...
Practice
Writing

14.7 THE SHUTTLE AND BEYOND
Reading
Discussion
Writing

14.8 IMAGINING LIFE IN SPACE
Free practice

14.1 DEGREES OF PROBABILITY

> **Language:** Expressing probability in predictions,
> using adjective + infinitive structures:
> e.g. He is likely to do it.
> Revision of adverbs for expressing
> probability in predictions (see
> Intermediate Unit 19):
> e.g. He will probably do it.

Presentation and practice

1 Before you begin the exercise, do some quick revision of predictions using adverbs. If necessary, write the different forms on the board:

He	will certainly/definitely will probably probably won't certainly/definitely won't	go there.

2 Briefly introduce the exercise by establishing what cable television is.
3 Working individually or in groups, students read the text, and then mark in the letter they think is most appropriate to each of the numbered sentences. The purpose of this is to check their comprehension of the *adjective + infinitive* structures in the text.
4 Go through the answers, dealing with any vocabulary problems as they arise.
  Answers: (1) A (2) D (3) C (4) B (5) A (6) A (7) C (8) B (9) A
5 Present the new structures by building up this table on the board:

He is	certain/sure/bound likely unlikely	to go there.

Point out:
i)   that these structures imply the future anyway, so they are used with the *present* tense of the verb *to be* (i.e. '*is* likely to...', not 'will be likely to...');
ii) that *likely* and *unlikely* are *adjectives*;
iii) that the structure 'is certain not to...' is possible, but hardly ever used;
iv) the formation of structures with *There is/are*:

There will certainly be There is certain to be	a lot of discussion.
There will probably be There are likely to be	a lot of people there.

Practice

1 Do the exercise with the class.
2 Divide the class into groups to discuss cable TV.
▶ W14 Ex 1 ◀

14.2 PRECAUTIONS   Practice

> **Language:** Practice of language introduced in 14.1.
> Practice of 'advice' structures (see Unit 8).

1 🔊 Play the examples on the tape. Demonstrate the pairwork by doing
   (1) with the whole class, and asking students to give as many different
   predictions as possible:
   e.g. Yes, you should – the restaurant's likely to be full.
                          – there are bound to be a lot of people there.
       There's no point – there are unlikely to be many people there.
                          – there's bound to be plenty of room.
2 Students have conversations in pairs, taking it in turns to ask the question.
3 As a round-up, ask different students what predictions they made.
▶ W14 Ex 2 ◀

14.3 HOROSCOPES   Writing

> **Language:** Free practice in making predictions, using
> infinitive structures, adverbs and modals.

1 Read the two horoscopes with the class. Introduce the exercise by sum-
   marising the range of prediction structures to be used.
2 Divide the class into five groups, and give each group two zodiac signs.
   Working together, they write two horoscopes similar to the ones they have
   read.
3 Each group reads out its horoscopes to the rest of the class.

14.4 CONDITIONAL   Presentation and practice 🔊
PREDICTIONS

> **Language:** 'Conditional' predictions, using: *If, Unless, As
> long as, Provided (that)...*
> Further practice of prediction structures.

This is a Listening Presentation. (See 'Dealing with listening' in Part 3.)

Part 1

A: Yes I think as things are at the moment we're in quite a lot of danger. Well, the trouble is...um...the two sides really need to talk a lot more, well see the other side's point of view, otherwise it does seem rather hopeless.

B: I think...um...that the balance of power is keeping us out of any real danger of war, I mean as things are at the moment neither side would really dare to start a war because of the consequences.

C: Well I think it's really a question of keeping dialogue going – you know the SALT talks – things like that. I think if that ever stopped altogether then well, we'd really have something to worry about.

D: Well I don't see any way out really, I mean it doesn't matter how much they talk about a deterrent, all the time they're making new weapons and eventually there are going to be so many weapons around that someone's going to start using them, it's inevitable.

Part 2

A: I think things are fairly well under control really – the only real danger is if someone starts a war accidentally.

B: The only thing I worry about is someone pressing the button before anyone can stop him – you know, some madman – otherwise I think we'll survive O.K.

C: The trouble is I think more and more countries are getting nuclear weapons and that's getting really dangerous. We've really got to stop nuclear weapons spreading.

D: Well obviously neither of the superpowers want to start a war. The only danger is if they both get drawn into a crisis on opposite sides.

E: Well, I really think the United Nations helps a lot because...er...it provides a place where people can talk. I think with the UN there countries would always stop short of an actual nuclear war.

1 Play Part 1 of the tape. Students match the remarks with the sentences. Establish that:

  i) *As long as* and *Provided (that)* mean the same as *If*, but are only used for *optimistic* predictions:

e.g. If

As long as	he works hard, he'll probably pass the exam.
Provided (that)	

(cf. If he's lazy, he may fail the exam.)

  ii) Like *If* and *Unless*, they are followed by the Present Simple tense, for talking about the future.

2 Point out the use of *should(n't)* meaning 'will probably (probably won't)'. *Note: should(n't)* is only used in 'optimistic' predictions.

3 Play Part 2 of the tape and ask students to summarise each remark, using a 'conditional' structure.

Possible answers: (A) (Optimistic). As long as no one starts a war accidentally, the world should remain fairly stable.

  (B) (Optimistic). Unless some madman presses the button, we'll probably survive.

  (C) (Pessimistic). If nuclear weapons spread to more countries, there's very likely to be a nuclear war.

  (D) (Optimistic). Provided the superpowers don't get drawn into a crisis on opposite sides, there shouldn't be a war.

(E) (Optimistic). As long as different countries can keep talking to each other, they will stop short of a nuclear war.

4 Divide the class into groups for the discussion.
5 Ask each group to summarise what conclusions they came to.
► W14 Ex 3 ◄

14.5   IN YOUR LIFETIME

> **Language:** Free practice of language introduced so far in this unit.

Free practice

1 Demonstrate the exercise by writing the first question and the scale on the board. Say what you think, then mark in your answer. Then ask various students what they think, and mark in their answers. Encourage them to talk freely about the question, making predictions and giving reasons:
   e.g. Well, I think the world's supply of oil is unlikely to run out for some time, because there are still huge oilfields that we haven't even started exploiting yet...
2 Divide the class into five groups, and assign each group a pair of questions. Give time for each group to answer their own two questions.
3 Students wander freely round the class, either individually or in pairs, asking their two questions and recording the answers they receive.
4 When they have finished, students return to their original groups to 'collate' their answers.
5 Ask each group to report their results to the rest of the class.

Writing

The writing can be done in class or for homework.
► W14 Ex 4 ◄

14.6   PREDICTING CONSEQUENCES

> **Language:** Contrast between:
>   i) Use of *will, is likely to*, etc. for *predicting* events and their consequences
>   ii) Use of *would*, for *imagining* alternative possibilities and their consequences (see 8.7 and 10.3).

Presentation

1 Read the letter. Check general comprehension by asking questions round the class:
e.g. What problem is the writer referring to?
Why does he think something should be done?
What is the Council planning to do?
Why doesn't the writer think they're right?
What's his solution?
Why does he think it's better?
2 Discuss the use of *will* and *would* in the letter. Establish that:
i) The writer uses *will* in the first two paragraphs (and other prediction structures) because he is talking about real plans and developments for the future.
ii) He uses *would* in the last paragraph because he is just *imagining* other possibilities. If necessary, refer students back to earlier examples of *would* in Units 8 and 10.

Practice

1 Divide the class into groups for the discussion. Either use the situations given or use similar 'local issues' that the class is familiar with.
2 Ask each group what conclusions they came to.

Writing

The writing can be done in class or for homework.
► W14 Ex 5 ◄

14.7 THE SHUTTLE AND BEYOND

Reading

For procedure, see 'Dealing with reading' in Part 3.
Answers: (1) (a) It can land again on Earth and is therefore reusable.
(b) It can transport passengers and large quantities of cargo; it can make frequent flights and there is no need to plan them far ahead.
(2) Transporting building materials and equipment to construct space stations.
(3) It would be much too large.
(4) A space station is a workplace; it is used for experimentation and further exploration in space. A space colony is a home; it is self-sufficient and large numbers of people live there permanently.
(5) It will be cheaper and more convenient.
(6) To make money from natural resources in space, and to increase military strength.

(7) (a) Vehicle for carrying goods backwards and forwards.
    (b) An experimental artificial world.
    (c) Requires nothing from outside.
    (d) Basic materials that are used to manufacture other things.

Discussion

Either use the questions as a basis for discussion with the whole class, or let students discuss them in groups and report their conclusions to the rest of the class afterwards.

Writing

The writing can be done in class or for homework.

14.8 IMAGING LIFE IN SPACE   Free practice

> **Language:** Free practice of language for 'imagining' (see 14.6 and also 10.3).

1 Demonstrate the groupwork by discussing one of the topics with the whole class.
2 Divide the class into groups for the activity.
3 As a round-up, ask each group what conclusions they came to about one of the topics.

Activities (following Unit 14)

STORY-TELLING

> **Language:** This activity draws on language from:
> Unit 3 (Relating past events)
> Unit 5 (Duration)
> Unit 6 (Reporting)
> Unit 11 (Events in sequence)
> and also Intermediate units concerned with
> Narration. (See Table 1 on p.3.)

1 Divide the class into pairs and give each pair a letter, A or B. Tell half the pairs to look only at the first half of the story (pictures 1 – 8) and the others to look only at the second half of the story (pictures 9 – 14). They work out how to tell the story in the past, including as much detail as possible.
2 Students form new pairs, so that each pair has one A and one B. Students tell each other the 'missing' half of the story.
3 As a check, ask students to tell the whole story round the class.

COMPOSITION

> **Language:** The composition is an extension of the previous
> activity, and draws on the same language.

The writing can be done in class or for homework.

Unit 15 News

This forms part of two series of units – those concerned with *narration* of past events and those concerned with relating *the past and the present*. It deals with language for announcing and giving details of news, and for reporting what one has heard from other people. This unit brings together the main tense uses practised in the Intermediate and Upper-Intermediate Courses.

The unit falls into two sections, followed by a general Free Practice exercise and a Reading Comprehension. The first section is concerned with announcing news and giving details of it; it practises Present Perfect, Present and Past tenses (Simple and Continuous). The second section is concerned with reporting things you have heard from other people; it practises *be supposed to* and other passive reporting verbs.

Assumed knowledge

Before beginning this unit, students should be familiar with:

Uses of Present Perfect Simple and Continuous (Intermediate Units 8, 15, Upper-Intermediate Units 1, 5).

Uses of Past Simple and Continuous (Intermediate Unit 12, Upper-Intermediate Unit 11).

Present and Past infinitive forms (Intermediate Unit 23, Upper-Intermediate Units 2, 7, 10).

15.1 THE NEWS   Presentation and practice 📼

> **Language:** Use of the following tenses in giving news of a
> recent event:
> i)   Present Perfect Simple
> ii) Past Simple and Continuous
> iii) Present Perfect Continuous.

This is a Listening Presentation. (See 'Dealing with listening' in Part 3.)

The time is four o'clock.
  Here is the news summary.
There has been a serious accident on the M6 motorway in Lancashire, in which at least six people have lost their lives. It happened early this morning near Preston when a coach carrying 45 passengers collided with a heavy lorry. Rescue operations have been going on throughout the day, and a section of the motorway has been closed to traffic.
Important talks have been taking place at 10 Downing Street today between the Prime Minister and Trade Union leaders. They have agreed to work together to find ways of combating inflation and reducing the present level of unemployment in British industry.
Meanwhile, the Government has failed to avert a national bus strike, and the bus drivers' union has announced that no buses will run from next Monday. The decision to go ahead with the strike was announced by a union spokesman at the end of a meeting earlier this afternoon during which Government representatives failed to persuade the union and the employers to agree on a new wage plan.
The forest fire in southern France: firemen from six different towns have been fighting all day to prevent the fire from spreading further. Latest reports say that the blaze has still not been brought under control, and that an estimated three million pounds' worth of damage has already been caused. Four people have died in the fire so far, and 20 more have been taken to hospital with burns and other injuries. The French Government has asked all tourists to avoid the area.
Police in Manchester have been continuing their search for the murderer of 71-year-old Mrs Jane Simpkins, who was found beaten to death in the kitchen of her home two days ago. Articles found at the murder scene have been taken away for examination by police experts, and the detective-superintendent in charge of the case has appealed for information from members of the public. This morning detectives began making house-to-house inquiries in the immediate neighbourhood.

1 Play the tape and discuss what each news item is about. (Do not go into details.)
2 Play the tape again, pausing after each item so that students can note down the answers to the questions.
3 Divide the class into five groups. Give each group one of the news items to reconstruct orally from their notes.

4 Ask each group to give the news item they have reconstructed, and play the tape again to compare. As you go through, make sure students are aware of the following uses of tenses in the broadcast:
   i) *Present Perfect* for announcing news of an event:
      e.g. There *has been* a serious accident on the M6.
   ii) *Past Simple and Continuous* for giving details about the event – the time, the place, the participants, the circumstances:
      e.g. It happen*ed* early this morning near Preston when a coach collid*ed* with a heavy lorry.
   iii) *Present Perfect Simple* for giving information about the event (and later events) that is still relevant to the present – its results, effects and consequences:
      e.g. A section of the motorway *has been* closed to traffic.
   iv) *Present Perfect Continuous* for talking about recent activities or activities that are still continuing:
      e.g. Important talks *have been* tak*ing* place at 10 Downing St.
      Rescue operations *have been* go*ing* on throughout the day.
   Note: How much detail you go into will depend on how difficult the students found it to reconstruct the news item.

15.2 HEADLINE NEWS

> **Language:** Practice of language introduced in 15.1.

Practice

1 Look at the headlines, and check that students understand what they mean. Establish what the 'announcing' sentence will be for each news item:
   e.g. Twenty people have been killed in a collision at London Airport.
   Emphasise that the headlines refer to today's (i.e. recent) news, so the 'announcing' sentence can use the Present Perfect (with no time mentioned).
2 Divide the class into groups. Either assign a different headline to each group, or let them choose their own.
3 Ask each group to give their news story.

Writing

The writing can be done in class or for homework.
► W15 Ex 1, Ex 4 ◄

15.3 LOCAL INTEREST   Practice

> **Language:** Practice of language introduced in 15.1, used
> for telling local or personal news, informally.
> Questions involving Past and Present Perfect
> tenses for finding out about details of news.

1 Look at the announcement, and get the class to ask as many questions as
they can:
e.g. i) About the event itself: When did it happen?
                                 Which bank was it?
                                 How much money did they take?
    ii) Since the event: Have they caught them yet?
                                 Has the bank opened again?
2 Give time for each group to prepare a story.
Note: Item (c) should be about a local hotel; items (d) and (e) should be
about a well-known local figure or someone known to the class.
3 Students wander freely round the class, telling their news to anyone they
like.

15.4 YOUR OWN NEWS   Free practice

> **Language:** Free practice of language introduced so far in
> this unit.
>
> *Note:* Exactly the same tense relationships apply to 'official'
> news (e.g. 15.1) and to 'everyday' personal news (e.g. 'My
> sister's bought a new house').

1 Demonstrate the groupwork by telling the class a piece of news yourself.
2 Divide the class into groups for the activity.
3 As a possible round-up, ask each group to tell their most interesting piece of
news to the rest of the class.

15.5 HEARSAY

> **Language:** Ways of indicating that information is based on
> 'hearsay' (i.e. what we have heard other
> people say or have read somewhere):
> i) Formulae:
> e.g. *Apparently, they say, I'm told...*
> ii) *be supposed to* + infinitive.
>
> *Note:* The Presentation stage of this exercise concentrates
> on the structure *supposed to*, as this is likely to be more
> difficult. The Practice stage gives an opportunity to use
> *supposed to* and the formulae.

Presentation

1 Look at the sentences. Establish what 'hearsay' is, and the two different ways of reporting it. If you think it is necessary, show how the structures are related by building up these tables on the board:

Formulae

Apparently They/people say I'm told I've heard	he'<u>s</u> terribly stingy he'<u>s</u> liv<u>ing</u> in Paris he'<u>s</u> just <u>got</u> engaged

be supposed to + infinitive

He's supposed to	<u>be</u> terribly stingy <u>be</u> liv<u>ing</u> in Paris <u>have</u> just <u>got</u> engaged

Point out that *be supposed to* is the *passive* form of the verb *suppose* (we cannot, however, say 'People suppose that he's staying'). It is followed by the same range of infinitive forms as modals (see Unit 7) and *seem* (see Unit 2).

2 Ask students to change the sentences:
e.g. (1) Elephants are supposed to have very long memories.

Practice

Either do the exercise with the whole class, or let students ask each other questions in groups and go through their answers afterwards.
▶ W15 Ex 2 ◀

15.6 PASSIVE REPORTING VERBS

Presentation and practice

> **Language:** Other passive reporting verbs used for giving 'second hand' information: *thought, reported, estimated, known, believed, said, alleged.*
>
> *Note:* These verbs are mainly used in a more formal style, e.g. radio or newspaper reports. They are especially used when the source of the information is 'people in general'.

1 Look at the situation and examples. Present the structures by giving an example of your own, and writing these sentences on the board:

ACTIVE:	People <u>think</u> (<u>that</u>) he's living in London.
PASSIVE (1):	<u>It is thought that</u> he's living in London.
PASSIVE (2):	<u>He is thought to</u> be living in London.

If necessary, do some basic practice of the structure by giving other active sentences, and asking students to change them into the two passive forms.

2 Do the exercise round the class, presenting the other passive reporting verbs as you go along.

Practice

Either ask for suggestions from the whole class, or let students construct an imaginary report in groups, which they can then give to the rest of the class.
▶ W15 Ex 3 ◀

15.7 TODAY'S NEWS   Free practice

> **Language:** Free practice of language introduced in this unit.

1 At the end of the previous lesson, tell students to read or listen to today's news carefully. You should do the same, and if possible get news headlines from the BBC.
2 Give one sentence to each group.
3 Working together, each group writes the complete news story.
4 Ask groups to read out their stories in turn.

15.8 CHEQUEBOOK JOURNALISM

Reading and discussion

Either deal with this as a normal Reading Comprehension (see notes on 'Dealing with reading' in Part 3), or adopt the following procedure:

1 Divide the class into three groups. Each group reads and looks at the questions for *one* of the three passages.
2 Students form new groups, so that each new group contains at least one student from each of the original groups. In turn students tell each other what their passage was about, and they answer the discussion questions.
3 Ask each group to say what conclusions they came to, and if you like, continue the discussion with the whole class.

  Answers: *Charles tapes – the storm grows*
  (1) They contained rude remarks about the Australian Prime Minister. They contained personal details about Prince Charles and Lady Diana.
  (2) (This is a discussion question.) Possible answers: (a) to get information

about what Prince Charles was doing; (b) so that they would be
published and embarrass the royal family.
(3) (This is a discussion question.) Possible answer: popular articles
about famous people, especially scandal.
(4) (a) He didn't have to make any effort to get them.
(b) (This is a discussion question.)

Queen's 'distaste' at press payments
(1) Journalists approaching people and offering them money for a story.
(2) She felt that it was wrong for the relatives of a murderer to be making
money from his crimes. The Queen sent her a letter in reply to her
own, because she sympathised with her.
(3) (This is a discussion question.) Possible answer: because the press are
only interested in the crime as a 'story' and in the money they can
make out of it.
(4) They are thinking of ways to make it illegal for newspapers to offer
money for stories in cases like this.

Manufacturing a news story
(1) They are encouraging youths to act violently by their presence, and in
some cases paying them to do so.
(2) 'Hearsay' from colleagues; police have seen it happen; he was told by
youths that it happens.
(3) (This is a discussion question.) Possible answer: to get a good news
story and pictures that make their paper sell.
(4) Because he thinks reporters and photographers should be objective.

Writing

The writing can be done in class or for homework.

Activities (following Unit 15)

THE FUTURE OF SANTA CLARA

> **Language:** This activity draws on language from:
> Unit 8 (Advantages and disadvantages)
> Unit 12 (Comparison)
> Unit 14 (Prediction)
> and also Intermediate units concerned with
> Action, Comparison and Explanation. (See
> Table 1 on p.3.)

1 Introduce the activity by establishing the situation, and making sure students understand what the diagram means. Briefly discuss how each of the lines might continue.
2 Divide the class into three (or six) groups to prepare for the discussion (in each group, all the students are either A or B or C).
3 Students form new groups, so that each new group contains at least one person from each original group. They discuss the problems.
4 Ask the 'chairman' from each group to summarise their discussion.

COMPOSITION

> **Language:** The composition is an extension of the previous
> activity, and draws on the same language.

The writing can be done in class or for homework.

SITUATIONS

> **Language:** The situations draw on language from Units
> 13, 14 and 15.

For procedure, see Activities following Unit 3.

Unit 16 Revision

This unit consists of activities which can be used as a basis for revision of the whole course (Intermediate and Upper-Intermediate books).

Each revision activity covers one of the general functional areas covered by the course, and so brings together related language from different units.

Suggested procedure for each activity

1 Before beginning the activity, do your own revision of relevant language areas (these are indicated below). This should take the form of quick questioning round the class, to remind students of language points they have covered and to pinpoint any areas that need special attention. It may be necessary to present some of these again, or to refer back to earlier units.
2 *Activity*: go through the activity with the whole class. Try to get students to use as much of the language you are revising as possible (see also individual notes below).
3 *Extension*: so that every student has a chance to practise the language, it is a good idea to repeat all or part of the activity in pairs or groups, where this is appropriate (see also individual notes below).
4 *Writing*: most of the activities are followed by a writing stage. This can be done in class or for homework.

16.1 DESCRIBING PEOPLE

> **Language:** This activity revises language from:
>
> Intermediate: Unit 3 (Jobs and routine)
> Unit 5 (Past events)
> Unit 11 (Likes and dislikes)
> Unit 13 (Leisure activities and skills)
>
> Upper-Intermediate: Unit 1 (Experience)
> Unit 2 (Appearance)
> Unit 4 (Attitudes and reactions)

1 Look at the photographs and discuss Questions (1) and (2) with the whole class.

2 Build up an imaginary description of one of the four people with the whole class.
3 Divide the class into groups to give similar descriptions of the other three people, assigning one photograph to each group.
4 Ask each group to give their description to the whole class. (The groupwork stage can also be done as a guessing game: each group secretly chooses any of the photos and the rest of the class guess from their description which photo they have chosen.)

16.2 TAKING AND DIRECTING ACTION

> **Language:** This activity revises language from:
>
> Intermediate: Unit 2 (Decisions and intentions)
> Unit 7 (Requests and offers)
> Unit 14 (Advice)
> Unit 18 (Obligation)
>
> Upper-Intermediate: Unit 8 (Advantages and disadvantages)
> Unit 13 (Processes)

1 Discuss with the whole class what A and B might say in each situation.
2 Students act out the six conversations in pairs.

16.3 COMPARING THE PAST AND THE PRESENT

> **Language:** This activity revises language from:
>
> Intermediate: Unit 8 (Recent actions and activities)
> Unit 9 (Comparison)
> Unit 10 (The past and the present)
>
> Upper-Intermediate: Unit 12 (Comparison)

Either: discuss both topics briefly with the whole class and let them continue the discussion in groups.
Or: discuss one of the topics in detail with the whole class and let them discuss the other topic in groups.

16.4 DESCRIBING PLACES

> **Language:** This activity revises language from:
>
> Intermediate: Unit 1 (Places)
> Unit 4 (Direction)
> Unit 13 (Leisure activities and skills)
> Unit 16 (Location)

1 Build up a description with the whole class.
2 If you like, divide the class into pairs and let them practise giving the description to each other (or let them choose another town to describe in the same way).

16.5 RECENT ACTIONS AND ACTIVITIES

> **Language:** This activity revises language from:
>
> Intermediate: Unit 6 (Talking about now)
> Unit 8 (Recent actions and activities)
> Unit 10 (The past and the present)
> Unit 15 (Origin and duration)
>
> Upper-Intermediate: Unit 15 (News)

1 Ask students to suggest things they might say for each topic area.
2 In pairs, students act out a conversation.

16.6   DESCRIBING A SCENE

> **Language:** The first part of this activity revises language from:
>
> Intermediate: Unit 6 (Talking about now)
> Unit 8 (Recent actions and activities)
> Unit 16 (Location)
> Unit 20 (Objects)
>
> Upper-Intermediate: Unit 2 (Appearance)
> Unit 7 (Deductions and explanations)
>
> The second part of the activity revises language from:
>
> Intermediate: Unit 12 (Events and circumstances)
>
> Upper-Intermediate: Unit 3 (Relating past events)
> Unit 11 (Events in sequence)

1 Discuss the picture with the whole class.
2 Divide the class into groups to imagine a story based on the picture.
3 Ask each group to tell their story to the class.

16.7   PROBLEMS AND SOLUTIONS

> **Language:** This activity revises language from:
>
> Intermediate: Unit 19 (Prediction)
> Unit 21 (Degree)
> Unit 23 (Criticising)
> Unit 24 (Explanations)
>
> Upper-Intermediate: Unit 8 (Advantages and disadvantages)
> Unit 14 (Prediction)

1 Discuss one of the pictures with the whole class.
2 Divide the class into groups to discuss one of the other pictures.
3 Ask each group what conclusions they came to.

16.8 NARRATION CHOICES

> **Language:** This activity revises language from:
>
> Intermediate: Unit 5 (Past events)
> Unit 12 (Events and circumstances)
> Unit 22 (Setting a scene)
>
> Upper-Intermediate: Unit 3 (Relating past events)
> Unit 5 (Duration)
> Unit 6 (Reporting)
> Unit 9 (Clarifying)
> Unit 11 (Events in sequence)

1 For this activity, divide the class into groups first as a preparation stage. Let each group choose one of the three topics and practise what they will say.
2 Ask one person from each group to retell their joke, conversation or story to the rest of the class.
3 If you like, repeat the activity, asking each group to choose a different topic from the one they chose before.

16.9 QUESTIONS

> **Language:** This activity revises Yes/No question forms, using all tenses. The second part revises the same Units as 16.8 (Narration choices) above.

Play the game with the whole class. Before you begin, explain to the students that:
1 The information is only a small part of what they need to know to understand the story.
2 To find out the whole story, they must ask you questions, but can *only* ask questions to which you can answer 'Yes', 'No' or 'We don't know'.
3 You will also tell them if what they have asked is important or not.

  Answer: The man is trying to give up smoking, but he gets desperate for a cigarette. He goes into a tobacconist's shop, comes out with a box (packet) of cigarettes. He opens it, intending to light one up, but decides not to have one. So he throws the box away, and walks down the street, smiling because of his will-power.

16.10   SPEECHES

Language: Although the speeches can of course use any language, they can be used to revise language from:

Upper-Intermediate: Unit 4 (Attitudes and reactions)
Unit 8 (Advantages and disadvantages)
Unit 10 (Wishes and regrets)
Unit 12 (Comparison)
Unit 13 (Processes)
Unit 14 (Prediction)

1 Give each student time to prepare his speech, making brief notes if he wishes.
2 Ask each student to give a speech in turn.

Appendix A: Student's Book cassette – contents

This is a list of all material that is recorded on the Student's Book cassette.

1.3	Have you ever...?	Listening Model
2.1	Judging from appearances	Recorded Example
2.5	Describing people	Listening Presentation
		Recorded Example
2.8	A stony home	Listening Comprehension
3.2	Previous events	Recorded Example
3.3	Previous activities and actions	Recorded Example
3.8	A night to remember	Listening Comprehension
4.1	Expressing attitudes	Listening Presentation
4.2	Verbs and adjectives	Recorded Example
4.4	If there's one thing...	Recorded Example
4.5	The way	Listening Presentation
5.1	How long?	Listening Presentation
5.4	How long does it take?	Listening Model
5.8	Top dogs	Listening Comprehension
6.2	Conflicting reports	Recorded Example
6.4	Kinds of statement	Listening Presentation
6.5	Influencing and taking action	Recorded Example
7.1	Must, might, may & can't	Listening Presentation
7.4	Deductions and reasons: 'If'	Recorded Examples
7.6	Explanations	Listening Model
8.1	Good and bad effects	Listening Presentation
8.2	Pros and cons	Recorded Example
8.5	Advising on a choice	Recorded Example
9.2	Getting further information	Recorded Example
9.4	Witness	Recorded Example
9.5	Making sure	Recorded Example
9.6	You've got it all wrong	Listening Model
9.9	Job interview	Listening Comprehension
10.1	I wish & If only	Recorded Example
10.2	Conflicting wishes	Recorded Example
10.3	Fantasies	Listening Model
10.5	Feeling sorry for yourself	Recorded Example
11.4	Getting the order right	Recorded Example
11.8	Twin stories	Listening Comprehension
12.3	Comparing prices	Recorded Example
12.5	What is it?	Listening Model
12.7	Not what I'd expected	Recorded Example
13.2	Emphasising the right order	Recorded Example
13.3	Giving instructions	Listening Model
13.8	Making your own wine	Listening Comprehension
14.2	Precautions	Recorded Example
14.4	Conditional predictions	Listening Presentation
15.1	The news	Listening Presentation

Appendix B: Drills

LAB SESSION 1 (UNITS 1–3)

Drill 1 Asking about experiences

Listen. / * Now you add the question.

I went to the Caribbean last summer.
Have you ever been to the Caribbean?

The police stopped me in the street yesterday.
Have you ever been stopped in the street by the police?

Someone picked my pocket on Tuesday.
Have you ever had your pocket picked?*

A motor bike hit me a month ago.
Have you ever been hit by a motor bike?

They published my letter in the paper.
Have you ever had a letter published in the paper?

I flew in a supersonic jet the other day.
Have you ever flown in a supersonic jet?

They interviewed me for a radio programme a few weeks ago.
Have you ever been interviewed for a radio programme?

My house was broken into the other week.
Have you ever had your house broken into?

A complete stranger kissed me in the street this morning.
Have you ever been kissed by a complete stranger in the street?

Drill 2 Familiarity and unfamiliarity

Jill has just gone to live abroad, and she's finding things rather strange.
Listen. / * Now you respond.

They drive on the right.
She's not used to driving on the right.

And they stare at her.
She's not used to being stared at.

There's not much water, so she can't have a bath every day.
She's used to having a bath every day.*

They drink strong black coffee.
She's not used to drinking strong black coffee.

They don't work in the afternoons.
She's used to working in the afternoons.

People take her to open-air restaurants.
She's not used to being taken to open-air restaurants.

Someone cleans her flat for her.
She's not used to having her flat cleaned for her.

She has her own private office.
She's not used to having her own private office.

They don't wait in queues.
She's used to waiting in queues.

Mosquitoes bite her.
She's not used to being bitten by mosquitoes.

Drill 3 Sense impressions

Listen. / * Now you respond.

Look at that man. Is he going to jump into the water?
He looks as if he's going to jump into the water.

Can I try some? Mm. Camembert, isn't it?
It tastes like Camembert.

What's wrong with your voice? Have you got a cold?
You sound as if you've got a cold.*

157

Your eyes are all red. Have you been crying?
You look as if you've been crying.

Let's have some of that cake. Mm. Delicious.
It tastes delicious.

Sh! Listen! Are they having an argument?
They sound as if they're having an argument.

(Sniff, sniff). That's petrol, isn't it?
It smells like petrol.

Look at them. Are they going to a fancy dress party?
They look as if they're going to a fancy dress party.

What's that noise? Gunfire?
It sounds like gunfire.

What's the matter? Have you seen a ghost?
You look as if you've seen a ghost.

Drill 4   Seem

There seems to be something wrong with Ben, and some of his friends are getting worried about him. Listen. / * Now you respond.

He's changed somehow.
He seems to have changed somehow.
It's as if he's dreaming all the time.
He seems to be dreaming all the time.

As far as I can tell, he doesn't recognise me any more.
He doesn't seem to recognise me any more.*

He's...well...he's behaving rather strangely.
He seems to be behaving rather strangely.

Although as far as I know, he isn't unhappy.
He doesn't seem unhappy.

I've got the feeling that he doesn't care about his appearance.
He doesn't seem to care about his appearance.

And he's lost interest in his work — wouldn't you say?
He seems to have lost interest in his work.

Mind you, he's doing a lot of reading, it seems.
He seems to be doing a lot of reading.

I get the impression that he knows something that we don't.
He seems to know something that we don't.

My impression is that he needs medical attention.
He seems to need medical attention.

Drill 5   Previous events

Listen. / * Now you respond.

Brian forgot to set his alarm, so he woke up late.
Brian woke up late because he had forgotten to set his alarm.

He woke up late, so he left the house in a hurry.
He left the house in a hurry because he had woken up late.*

He left the house in a hurry, so he left his wallet at home.
He left his wallet at home because he had left the house in a hurry.

He left his wallet at home, so he went back home again.
He went back home again because he had left his wallet at home.

He went back home again, so he missed his bus.
He missed his bus because he had gone back home again.

He missed his bus, so he took a taxi.
He took a taxi because he had missed his bus.

He took a taxi, so he got to work early.
He got to work early because he had taken a taxi.

He got to work early, so he couldn't get in.
He couldn't get in because he had got to work early.

He couldn't get in, so he had some breakfast in a café.
He had some breakfast in a café because he hadn't been able to get in.

Drill 6   Previous activities

When Helen came home last night, she found that her children had been doing all sorts of things. She told a friend about it. Listen. / * Now you're the friend.

Well, there were some cards on the table.
Ah, so they'd been playing cards, had they?

And most of my chocolates were missing.
Ah, so they'd been eating your chocolates, had they?*

And the television was warm.
Ah, so they'd been watching television, had they?

And the ashtray was full of cigarette ends.
Ah, so they'd been smoking, had they?

Their breath smelled of whisky.
Ah, so they'd been drinking whisky, had they?

And my diary was open.
Ah, so they'd been reading your diary, had they?

And their dirty fingermarks were all over the telephone.
Ah, so they'd been using the telephone, had they?

There were even bicycle tyre marks on the carpet.
Ah, so they'd been riding their bicycles on the carpet, had they?

They seemed very happy.
Ah, so they'd been enjoying themselves, had they?

LAB SESSION 2 (UNITS 4–6)

Drill 1   Attitudes

Listen. / * Now you respond.

I like men with long beards. They impress me.
I see. So you find men with long beards impressive.

I don't like shy men. They irritate me.
I see. So you find shy men irritating.*

I don't like men with greasy hair. They disgust me.
I see. So you find men with greasy hair disgusting.

I like men with a good suntan. They really attract me.
I see. So you find men with a good suntan really attractive.

I don't like men who use bad language. They offend me.
I see. So you find men who use bad language offensive.

I like old-fashioned men. They amuse me.
I see. So you find old-fashioned men amusing.

I like intellectual men. They're interesting to talk to.
I see. So you find intellectual men interesting to talk to.

I don't like people who talk about their attitudes. They bore me.
I see. So you find people who talk about their attitudes boring.

Drill 2   Strong feelings

Listen. / * Now you respond.

Susan doesn't pay back her debts. She makes me angry.
If there's one thing that makes me angry, it's people who don't pay back their debts.

Tom has bad breath. I can't stand him.
If there's one thing I can't stand, it's people who have bad breath.*

Jack doesn't help with the housework. It makes me cross.
If there's one thing that makes me cross, it's people who don't help with the housework.

Alan smokes all the time. I hate it.
If there's one thing I hate, it's people who smoke all the time.

Anna doesn't keep her promises. She upsets me.
If there's one thing that upsets me, it's people who don't keep their promises.

Fiona never pays for anything. She gets on my nerves.
If there's one thing that gets on my nerves, it's people who never pay for anything.

Fred is always late for appointments. He annoys me.
If there's one thing that annoys me, it's people who are always late for appointments.

Pamela doesn't reply to letters. I really dislike her.
If there's one thing I really dislike, it's people who don't reply to letters.

Leo is only interested in himself. He makes me angry.
If there's one thing that makes me angry, it's people who are only interested in themselves.

Drill 3   Take and spend

Listen. / * Now you respond.

I did the washing in 20 minutes.
It took me 20 minutes to do the washing.

He watched television the whole evening.
He spent the whole evening watching television.*

She gets to the station in half an hour.
It takes her half an hour to get to the station.

He cut my hair in 10 minutes.
It took him 10 minutes to cut my hair.

On Sundays I sit in the garden for a couple of hours.
On Sundays, I spend a couple of hours sitting in the garden.

She's going to live in a tent for the next five days.
She's going to spend the next five days living in a tent.

I'm going to finish this book in three hours.
It's going to take me three hours to finish this book.

He worked in Africa for four years.
He spent four years working in Africa.

She usually does the crossword in 15 minutes.
It usually takes her 15 minutes to do the crossword.

He talks on the telephone for most of his working day.
He spends most of his working day talking on the telephone.

Drill 4   How long?

Listen. / * Now you respond.

I once lived in Russia, you know.
How long did you live in Russia?

I think he's ill.
How long has he been ill?

They're coming to stay next week.
How long are they staying?*

She used to work for the BBC.
How long did she work for the BBC?

We've got a dog.
How long have you had a dog?

She's writing her autobiography.
How long has she been writing her autobiography?

I'm on holiday from next Monday.
How long are you on holiday?

We used to have a dog.
How long did you have a dog?

He's a vegetarian.
How long has he been a vegetarian?

Drill 5   Reported speech

You went to a fortune-teller yesterday, and now you're telling a friend what the fortune-teller told you. Listen. / * Now you respond.

You were born abroad.
She told me that I had been born abroad.

Your lucky number is seven.
She told me that my lucky number was seven.*

You're going to be very famous one day.
She told me that I was going to be very famous one day.

You haven't met the person you're going to marry.
She told me that I hadn't met the person I was going to marry.

You've been worrying too much about something.
She told me that I had been worrying too much about something.

You aren't ambitious enough.
She told me that I wasn't ambitious enough.

By next year you will be living abroad.
She told me that by next year I would be living abroad.

You don't believe what I've told you.
She told me that I didn't believe what she had told me.

You're going to change your mind.
She told me that I was going to change my mind.

Drill 6   Reporting verbs

Last night, a government minister spoke on TV. Listen. / * Now you report what the minister said.

Difficult times lie ahead. (warn)
He warned us that difficult times lay ahead.

I know – I know – we haven't carried out all our election promises. (admit)
He admitted that they hadn't carried out all their election promises.*

We are still trying to correct the mistakes of the previous government. (claim)
He claimed that they were still trying to correct the mistakes of the previous government.

The previous government ruined the country's economy. (accuse)
He accused the previous government of ruining the country's economy.

The government will rebuild the economy. (assure)
He assured us that the government would rebuild the economy.

We will create new jobs. (promise)
He promised to create new jobs.

Unemployment figures are already going down. (point out)
He pointed out that unemployment figures were already going down.

But this can only continue if the country works together. (warn)
He warned us that this could only continue if the country worked together.

We are not afraid of the difficult road ahead. (deny)
He denied that they were afraid of the difficult road ahead.

LAB SESSION 3 (UNITS 7–9)

Drill 1   Making deductions

Listen. / * Now you make the deductions.

— *Surely they knew we were coming.*
— *Well, perhaps they didn't get our letter.*
So they might not have known we were coming, then.

— *He's a maths teacher, isn't he?*
— *Well, he did English at university.*
So he can't be a maths teacher, then.

— *Surely they haven't gone out.*
— *Well, they're not answering the telephone.*
So they must have gone out, then.*

— *Surely she's not going abroad for her holiday.*
— *Well, she's had an increase in salary.*
So she might be going abroad for her holiday, then.

— *She's not married, is she?*
— *Well, she's wearing a wedding ring.*
So she must be married, then.

— *Surely he's woken up.*
— *Well, I can hear snoring coming from his room.*
So he can't have woken up, then.

— *They weren't lying, were they?*
— *Well, they're not entirely honest, you know.*
So they might have been lying, then.

— *He's been doing well at work, hasn't he?*
— *Well, actually he's just been given the sack.*
So he can't have been doing well at work, then.

— *Surely they're coming.*
— *Well, they said they weren't sure.*
So they might not be coming, then.

Drill 2   Giving reasons for deductions

Listen. / * Now you respond.

The lights are on, so they must be at home.
That's right. If they weren't at home, the lights wouldn't be on.

Their car's there, so they can't have left.
That's right. If they had left, their car wouldn't be there.*

The shops are open, so it can't be Sunday.
That's right. If it was Sunday, the shops wouldn't be open.

He's smiling, so he must be happy.
That's right. If he wasn't happy, he wouldn't be smiling.

She's got the job, so she must be good.
That's right. If she wasn't good, she wouldn't have got the job.

They haven't phoned, so they can't be in trouble.
That's right. If they were in trouble, they would have phoned.

He didn't buy it, so he can't have liked it.
That's right. If he'd liked it, he would have bought it.

She's gone to work, so she can't be ill.
That's right. If she was ill, she wouldn't have gone to work.

He employs an interpreter, so he doesn't speak Arabic.
That's right. If he spoke Arabic, he wouldn't employ an interpreter.

Drill 3   Effects

Lillian is talking about the history of women in society. Listen. / * Now you respond.

Women couldn't get good jobs.
Tradition made it difficult.
Tradition made it difficult for women to get good jobs.

Women didn't get promoted. Employers prevented them.
Employers prevented women from getting promoted.*

Girls didn't take scientific subjects.
Schools discouraged them.
Schools discouraged girls from taking scientific subjects.

Girls married young and had children.
Parents encouraged them.
Parents encouraged girls to marry young and have children.

And they didn't go out to work. Their husbands stopped them.
Their husbands stopped them from going out to work.

But later many women got jobs. Financial problems forced them to.
Financial problems forced many women to get jobs.

They didn't do housework all day. New technology saved them from that.
New technology saved them from doing housework all day.

Women were able to compete with men for good jobs. Changing attitudes allowed them to.
Changing attitudes allowed women to compete with men for good jobs.

Nowadays employers have to treat men and women equally. The law forces them to.
Nowadays the law forces employers to treat men and women equally.

But women are not completely equal. Prejudice still prevents that.
Prejudice still prevents women from being completely equal.

Drill 4   Don't do it

Listen. / * Now you give the advice.

There's no petrol. (try to start the car)
It's no use trying to start the car.

We're nearly there now. (catch a bus)
It's not worth catching a bus.

We wouldn't watch it much anyway. (buy a new TV)
It's not worth buying a new TV.*

Nobody can hear you. (shout for help)
It's no use shouting for help.

I've made up my mind. (try to make me change my mind)
It's no use trying to make me change my mind.

It didn't cost much anyway. (take it back to the shop)
It's not worth taking it back to the shop.

They'll refuse to change it anyway. (take it back to the shop)
It's no use taking it back to the shop.

We won't be there for very long. (take sandwiches)
It's not worth taking sandwiches.

I don't smoke. (ask me for a cigarette)
It's no use asking me for a cigarette.

Drill 5   Getting it right

Listen. / * Now you respond.

Do you remember that Chinese restaurant we went to last summer?
It was Japanese.
Of course, it was a Japanese restaurant we went to, wasn't it?

The Andrews recommended it, didn't they?
It was the Browns.
Of course, it was the Browns who recommended it, wasn't it?

We had raw meat, didn't we?
It was raw fish.
Of course, it was raw fish we had, wasn't it?

And didn't we meet the Joneses there?
It was the Smiths.
Of course, it was the Smiths we met there, wasn't it?

And we all went to a pub afterwards, didn't we?
It was a nightclub.
Of course, it was a nightclub we went to afterwards, wasn't it?

And I spilt my drink over a waiter.
It was a waitress.
Of course, it was a waitress I spilt my drink over, wasn't it?

And the barman asked us to leave.
It was the manager.
Of course, it was the manager who asked us to leave, wasn't it?

And I drove us home, didn't I?
I did.
Of course, it was you who drove us home, wasn't it?

Aren't we going to a Japanese restaurant tonight?
Chinese.
Of course, it's a Chinese restaurant we're going to tonight, isn't it?

Drill 6   Reported questions

Linda has been looking at a room to let. While she was there, the landlady asked her a lot of questions. Linda is telling a friend about it. Listen. / * Now you report the questions.

Are you married?
She asked me if I was married.

What are you studying?
She wanted to know what I was studying.*

Have you got any children?
She asked me if I had any children.

Have you ever lived away from home before?
She wanted to know if I had ever lived away from home before.

How long are you planning to stay in London?
She asked me how long I was planning to stay in London.

Do you know many people in London?
She asked me if I knew many people in London.

How long have you been looking for a place to live?
She wanted to know how long I had been looking for a place to live.

When do you want to move in?
She asked me when I wanted to move in.

How much can you afford to pay?
She wanted to know how much I could afford to pay.

LAB SESSION 4 (UNITS 10–12)

Drill 1   Making wishes

Dorothy is unhappy about being so young, and wishes things were different. Listen. / * Now you make the wishes.

I'm so young.
I wish I wasn't so young.

I can't leave school.
I wish I could leave school.

My parents won't listen to me.
I wish my parents would listen to me.*

I'm not old enough to drive.
I wish I was old enough to drive.

People call me Dotty instead of Dorothy.
I wish people didn't call me Dotty instead of Dorothy.

My parents don't treat me like an adult.
I wish my parents treated me like an adult.

I have to share my room with my sister.
I wish I didn't have to share my room with my sister.

I'm not earning any money.
I wish I was earning some money.

I can't run away from home.
I wish I could run away from home.

Drill 2   Regrets and explanations

Listen. / * Now you respond.

What a fool I was not to park in the car park.
I wish I'd parked in the car park.

Yes, they took your car away, didn't they?
Exactly. If I'd parked in the car park, they wouldn't have taken my car away.*

How stupid I was not to wear a tie.
I wish I'd worn a tie.

Yes, they didn't let you in, did they?
Exactly. If I'd worn a tie, they would have let me in.

Why on earth was I so rude?
I wish I hadn't been so rude.

Yes, he hit you, didn't he?
Exactly. If I hadn't been so rude, he wouldn't have hit me.

I should have been wearing a seat belt.
I wish I'd been wearing a seat belt.

Yes, you hurt your head, didn't you?
Exactly. If I'd been wearing a seat belt, I wouldn't have hurt my head.

Whatever made me invest in silver?
I wish I hadn't invested in silver.

Yes, you lost all your money, didn't you?
Exactly. If I hadn't invested in silver, I wouldn't have lost all my money.

Drill 3   Did or had done?

Listen. / * Now you say what happened.

I sat down and I read my letters.
When I had sat down I read my letters.

I sat down and the chair collapsed.
When I sat down the chair collapsed.*

He switched on the television and there was an explosion.
When he switched on the television there was an explosion.

He switched on the television and he ate his dinner.
When he had switched on the television he ate his dinner.

I heard the news and I was upset.
When I heard the news I was upset.

I heard the news and I turned off the radio.
When I had heard the news I turned off the radio.

She got out of the car and she locked it.
When she had got out of the car she locked it.

She got out of the car and she was surrounded by photographers.
When she got out of the car she was surrounded by photographers.

The burglars broke into the house and they woke me up.
When the burglars broke into the house they woke me up.

The burglars broke into the house and they began looking for the money.
When the burglars had broken into the house they began looking for the money.

Drill 4   No sooner...

Jacqueline went on a camping holiday last year, but it wasn't long before things started going wrong. Listen. / * Now you respond.

She picked up her case and immediately the handle broke.
No sooner had she picked up her case than the handle broke.

She got onto the motorway and immediately her car broke down.
No sooner had she got onto the motorway than her car broke down.*

She arrived at the camp site and immediately it started pouring with rain.
No sooner had she arrived at the camp site than it started pouring with rain.

She put up her tent and the wind immediately blew it down.
No sooner had she put up her tent than the wind blew it down.

She lit her stove and it immediately ran out of gas.
No sooner had she lit her stove than it ran out of gas.

She started reading and immediately her lamp went out.
No sooner had she started reading than her lamp went out.

She fell asleep and immediately some dogs started barking.
No sooner had she fallen asleep than some dogs started barking.

She went to the beach and the sun immediately went in.
No sooner had she gone to the beach than the sun went in.

She drove home again, and immediately the weather improved.
No sooner had she driven home again than the weather improved.

Drill 5   Big and small differences

Listen. / * Now you make the comparisons.

Is May or June hotter in England?
(slightly)
June is slightly hotter than May.

Which is cheaper – gold or silver?
(considerably)
Silver is considerably cheaper than gold.

Do men live longer than women?
(not quite)
Men don't live quite as long as women.*

Which takes longer – going by train or
going by plane? (much)
Going by train takes much longer than
going by plane.

How big is the moon compared with the
earth? (not nearly)
The moon isn't nearly as big as the
earth.

Which is heavier – a pound or a
kilogram? (far)
A kilogram is far heavier than a pound.

Is England or Scotland colder? (slightly)
Scotland is slightly colder than England.

An ordinary year is longer than a leap
year, isn't it? (not quite)
An ordinary year isn't quite as long as a
leap year.

How expensive is second class compared
with first class? (not nearly)
Second class isn't nearly as expensive as
first class.

Drill 6   Not what I expected

Sasha visited London for the first time
last year. He's telling a friend about it.
Listen. / * Now you respond.

London was big. I'd expected it to be
smaller.
London was bigger than I'd expected it
to be.

I'd thought it would be very cold. But it
wasn't.
It wasn't as cold as I'd thought it would
be.*

The shops were expensive. I'd hoped
they would be cheaper.
The shops were more expensive than I'd
hoped they would be.

The hotel wasn't very nice. It should
have been nicer.
The hotel wasn't as nice as it should
have been.

The language was easy. I'd expected it
to be more difficult.
The language was easier than I'd
expected it to be.

I'd been told London was dirty. But it
wasn't, really.
London wasn't as dirty as I'd been told
it was.

I spent a lot of money. I shouldn't have
done.
I spent more money than I should have
done.

The people were friendly. But I'd hoped
they would be friendlier.
The people weren't as friendly as I'd
hoped they would be.

I know a lot of English now. I didn't
before I went to London.
I know more English now than I did
before I went to London.

LAB SESSION 5 (UNITS 13–15)

Drill 1   Getting the order right

Listen. / * Now you give the advice.

Touch a chess piece – decide where to move.
You should decide where to move before you touch a chess piece.
Or in other words...
You shouldn't touch a chess piece until you've decided where to move. *

Start on a long drive – check your tyres.
You should check your tyres before you start on a long drive.
Or in other words...
You shouldn't start on a long drive until you've checked your tyres.

Taste your meal – put salt on it.
You should taste your meal before you put salt on it.
Or in other words...
You shouldn't put salt on your meal until you've tasted it.

Do an exercise – look at the examples.
You should look at the examples before you do an exercise.
Or in other words...
You shouldn't do an exercise until you've looked at the examples.

Shake the bottle – pour out the sauce.
You should shake the bottle before you pour out the sauce.
Or in other words...
You shouldn't pour out the sauce until you've shaken the bottle.

Drill 2   The Passive in describing processes

A postman is explaining how letters reach their destination. Listen. / * Now you respond.

Well, first we collect the letters from the letter boxes.
First the letters are collected from the letter boxes.

And then we take them to the sorting office.
When they've been collected from the letter boxes, they're taken to the sorting office.

Then we stamp on the postmarks.
When they've been taken to the sorting office, the postmarks are stamped on. *

And then we sort the letters.
When the postmarks have been stamped on, the letters are sorted.

And then we send them to their destination post offices.
When they've been sorted, they are sent to their destination post offices.

Then we sort them into streets.
When they've been sent to their destination post offices, they're sorted into streets.

Then we tie them up.
When they've been sorted into streets, they're tied up.

And we put them into mailbags.
When they've been tied up they're put into mailbags.

Then we give them to the postman.
When they've been put into mailbags, they're given to the postman.

Then he delivers them to their destinations.
When they've been given to the postman, they're delivered to their destinations.

Drill 3   Probabilities

The staff of the London underground trains are starting a strike tomorrow. A transport official is being interviewed about what he thinks will happen. Listen. / * Now you respond.

– Do you think a lot of people will be late for work tomorrow?
– Oh yes, this is bound to happen.
A lot of people are bound to be late for work tomorrow.

– What about buses? Will the transport authorities provide extra buses?
– Very unlikely, I'd say.
The transport authorities are very unlikely to provide extra buses. *

— *So there'll be long queues at the bus stops tomorrow, then?*
— *Oh certainly, certainly.*
There are certain to be long queues at the bus stops tomorrow.

— *The Union is demanding a big pay increase. Do you think the Transport Authorities will pay the increase?*
— *This is unlikely, in my view.*
The Transport Authorities are unlikely to pay the increase.

— *So the strike will last for some time, you think?*
— *Yes, this is likely.*
The strike is likely to last for some time.

— *What about traffic? Surely there'll be more cars on the roads than usual?*
— *Yes, that's certain.*
There are certain to be more cars on the road than usual.

— *So there'll be traffic jams in the centre?*
— *Yes, this is sure to happen, I'm afraid.*
There are sure to be traffic jams in the centre.

— *Aren't people going to be angry with the strikers?*
— *I'd say that was very likely, wouldn't you?*
People are very likely to be angry with the strikers.

— *Is there any possibility that the strike will be called off?*
— *That's unlikely to happen.*
The strike is unlikely to be called off.

Drill 4   Conditional predictions

Listen. / * Now you make the predictions.

You're sure to get there on time – but you'll have to hurry. (provided)
Provided that you hurry, you're sure to get there on time.

If you want to sell it, you'll have to repair it first. (unless)
Unless you repair it first, you won't sell it.*

I hope nothing goes wrong. Then we should win. (provided)
Provided that nothing goes wrong, we should win.

Obey my instructions. Otherwise you might get hurt. (if)
If you don't obey my instructions, you might get hurt.

Listen carefully. Otherwise you're certain to misunderstand. (unless)
Unless you listen carefully, you're certain to misunderstand.

That car will last for years – but you must look after it. (as long as)
As long as you look after it, that car will last for years.

He's unlikely to bite – but don't frighten him. (provided)
Provided that you don't frighten him, he's unlikely to bite.

He should stay in bed for a few days – then he'll be all right. (as long as)
As long as he stays in bed for a few days, he'll be all right.

I wish you'd slow down – there's bound to be an accident otherwise. (unless)
Unless you slow down, there's bound to be an accident.

Drill 5   Headline news

This last drill is a little different. You will hear three news items. Listen to each news item, and make sentences from the prompts given on the Drills pages.
Here's Item 1:

A London man has made a strange discovery – which could make him rich. Tim Johnson, a taxi driver, was cleaning his taxi this morning when he noticed a bag on the floor. When he opened the bag, he found half a million pounds. Mr Johnson took the bag straight to the police, who are now trying to find the person who left the bag in the taxi. They have talked to several of Mr Johnson's customers, but so far no one has claimed the money. All of which suits Mr Johnson: if the money is not claimed within six months, it will go to him.

Now make sentences from the prompts.

1 (*Pause*) A London man has made a strange discovery.
2 Tim Johnson was cleaning his taxi when he noticed a bag on the floor.
3 When he opened the bag, he found half a million pounds.
4 He took the bag straight to the police.
5 The police are trying to find the person who left the bag in the taxi.
6 They have talked to several of Mr Johnson's customers.
7 So far no one has claimed the money.
8 If the money is not claimed within six months, it will go to Mr Johnson.

Now listen to Item 2:

There have been more problems with the London underground today. Two hundred people were trapped for two hours this morning in a rush hour train. The train was taking people to work in central London when it stopped between stations. It took nearly two hours to repair the trouble. Twenty passengers were taken to hospital suffering from shock, but most of them were later allowed to go home.

Now make sentences from the prompts.

1 There have been more problems with the London underground today.
2 Two hundred people were trapped for two hours this morning in a rush-hour train.
3 The train was taking people to work when it stopped between stations.

4 It took nearly two hours to repair the trouble.
5 Twenty passengers were taken to hospital suffering from shock.
6 Most of them were later allowed to go home.

Now listen to Item 3:

Police have arrested the owner of a video shop in Piccadilly. Martin Weeks, who is 35, was arrested yesterday and charged with selling illegal video tapes. The tapes are said to be home-made copies of the new American film, *Lost Country*, which has not yet been shown in British cinemas. *Lost Country* has broken box-office records in America, and about 4,000 illegal copies of the film are thought to have been sold in Britain. Mr Weeks will appear in court on Monday.

Now make sentences from the prompts.

1 Police have arrested the owner of a video shop in Piccadilly.
2 Martin Weeks was arrested yesterday.
3 He was charged with selling illegal video tapes.
4 The tapes are said to be illegal copies of *Lost Country*.
5 *Lost Country* has not yet been shown in British cinemas.
6 *Lost Country* has broken box-office records in America.
7 4,000 illegal copies of the film are thought to have been sold in Britain.
8 Mr Weeks will appear in court on Monday.

Appendix C: Guide to test answers

These notes are intended as a guide to marking (and going through in class) the answers to the Progress Tests and the Final Achievement Test. The answers given should be treated as a guide only, since many of the test questions allow a fairly wide range of 'correct' answers. In some cases (e.g. the Sentence Rewriting sections) the student needs to keep very close to the answers given. Where a wider range of answers is possible, the answer given is preceded by 'e.g.' to show that it is only one of a number of possibilities. Answers are not given for the Composition sections: these should be judged on how successfully the student uses appropriate language to talk about the topic.

PROGRESS TEST UNITS 1–3

1 Sentence rewriting   *1½ marks for each answer*

(1) Have you ever been shouted at?
(2) This is the first time he's (ever) been out with a girl.
(3) Our children are used to going to school by bus.
(4) I've never had my wallet stolen (by anyone).

2 Appearances   *1 mark for each answer*

(1) He seems to have lived on his own most of his life.
(2) It sounds as if/though someone's knocking the wall down.
(3) This painting looks like / looks as if it is a genuine Rembrandt.
(4) He seems to have terrible personal problems.
(5) They look as if/though they're enjoying themselves.

3 Gap-filling   *1 mark for each answer*

(1) (quite) used to
(2) had been playing
(3) e.g. had been sleeping peacefully
(4) his early forties

4 Tenses   *½ mark for each answer*

(1)	have been sailing	(11)	started
(2)	have come	(12)	woke
(3)	have ever been	(13)	saw
(4)	was	(14)	coming
(5)	was sailing	(15)	knew
(6)	was	(16)	was
(7)	was	(17)	had heard
(8)	was	(18)	had erupted
(9)	hadn't slept	(19)	hadn't paid
(10)	had been	(20)	was / had been

170

5 Vocabulary   *½ mark for each answer*

(1) snub nose   (4) pale complexion
(2) bushy eyebrows   (5) wavy hair
(3) cleft chin   (6) full lips

6 Composition   *6 marks for each paragraph*

PROGRESS TEST UNITS 4–6

1 Sentence rewriting   *1½ marks for each answer*

(1) John said that he would come if he had enough time.
(2) She told me that I was the nastiest person she'd ever met.
(3) It took him half an hour to do (all) the shopping.
(4) I found his performance very impressive.
(5) What I hate about Peter is the way he shouts all the time. / What I hate is the way Peter shouts all the time.
(6) If there's one thing that really gets on my nerves it's people who don't say thank you.

2 Reporting   *1 mark for each answer*

(1) e.g. He suggested that I should go and see my bank manager.
(2) e.g. He accused us of talking about him behind his back.
(3) e.g. She assured him that he would be in absolutely no danger at all.
(4) e.g. They threatened to make life very difficult for us if we didn't cooperate.
(5) e.g. He begged them to take him away from there.
(6) e.g. She denied taking my typewriter.

3 Gap-filling   *1 mark for each answer*

(1) e.g. I like most about him is
(2) e.g. was rather disappointed
(3) e.g. it was nearly three o'clock
(4) e.g. on what kind of mood I'm in

4 How long?   *1 mark for each answer*

(1) e.g. How long have you been smoking a pipe (for)?
(2) e.g. How long will you stay / will you be staying in France?
(3) e.g. How long did the party go on for?
(4) e.g. How long does it take you to get to college?

5 Vocabulary   *½ mark for each answer*

(1) (a) scared/frightened/terrified   (2) (a) mean/stingy
    (b) bored   (b) frivolous/cheerful
    (c) irritated/annoyed/bored   (c) pessimistic
    (d) annoyed/upset/offended   (d) credulous/gullible
                                             (e) irritable/bad-tempered/short-tempered
                                             (f) sociable

6 Composition   *6 marks for each paragraph*

171

PROGRESS TEST UNITS 7–9

1 Sentence rewriting   *1½ marks for each answer*

(1) Having a sun-lamp enables/allows you to get a tan whenever you like.
(2) Having bars on your windows prevents/stops people (from) breaking into your house.
(3) She asked me if I had ever been invited to a fancy dress party.
(4) Jack was the person (who/that) I lent my bicycle to, wasn't he?
(5) Can you remember if/whether he bought a typewriter?
(6) The trouble with records is that they get scratched so easily.

2 Deductions   *1 mark for each answer*

(1) (i) He can't have gone abroad.
   (ii) If he had gone abroad, he would have taken his passport with him.
(2) (i) She must like me.
   (ii) If she didn't like me, she wouldn't have bought me flowers.
(3) (i) He must be still working.
   (ii) If he'd finished working, he would have come home by now.
(4) (i) He can't have been swimming.
   (ii) If he'd been swimming, his hair would be wet.

3 Advice/suggestions   *1 mark for each answer*

(1) There's no point in inviting him – he never goes to parties.
(2) We might as well watch TV – there's nothing else to do.
(3) We ought to open a bank account – it isn't safe to keep all our money under the bed.
(4) You ought not to go swimming – you'll make your cold worse.

4 Gap-filling   *1 mark for each answer*

(1) e.g. you joined a sports club
(2) e.g. doesn't necessarily mean that
(3) e.g. What flavour yoghurt
(4) get engaged to?

5 Vocabulary   *¼ mark for each word*

(1) (a) e.g. boil, fry, bake
   (b) e.g. arson, burglary, murder
   (c) e.g. broken it, bruised it, burnt it
(2) (a) all *ranks* in the army
   (b) all *shades* of red
   (c) all items of *furniture*

6 Composition   *6 marks for each paragraph*

PROGRESS TEST UNITS 10–12

1 Sentence rewriting *1½ marks for each answer*

(1) Doing tests isn't nearly as interesting as having lessons.
(2) Our balcony isn't quite as big as yours / isn't much smaller than yours.
(3) If I had gone to university, I wouldn't be doing this job now.
(4) When I had written the address, I stuck the stamp on the envelope.
(5) She didn't start using the machine before/until she had read the instructions.
(6) No sooner had I hung out the washing than it started to rain.

2 Wishes and regrets *1 mark for each answer*

(1) e.g. (i) I wish I'd walked up the stairs.
      (ii) I wish I had a torch.
(2) e.g. (i) If only she would write to me.
      (ii) I wish I was with her.
(3) e.g. (i) I wish someone would come along the road.
      (ii) If only I knew more about engines.
(4) e.g. (i) If only I could house-train it.
      (ii) I wish I'd bought a cat instead.

3 Comparison *1½ marks for each answer*

(1) Petrol costs nearly/almost three times as much as it used to. / Petrol is nearly/almost three times as expensive as it used to be.
(2) Home-made wine is a fifth (of) the price of shop wine. / Home-made wine costs a fifth as much as shop wine.
(3) He stayed out considerably longer/later than he should have done.
(4) It wasn't quite as hot / The temperature wasn't quite as high as I expected (it to be).

4 Gap-filling *1 mark for each answer*

(1) e.g. I'd hand it in to the police
(2) e.g. have walked to work
(3) shouldn't have
(4) e.g. have lent you some
(5) e.g. as I set eyes on her

5 Composition *6 marks for each paragraph*

PROGRESS TEST UNITS 13–15

1 Sentence rewriting *1½ marks for each answer*

(1) You shouldn't buy a car before/until you've learnt to drive.
(2) When the corn has been cut, it is stored in a dry place.
(3) As long as we aren't delayed at the airport, we'll take off on time.
(4) He's supposed to have left home at the age of 14.
(5) She's supposed to be earning £20,000 a year.
(6) Fireworks are generally believed to have been invented by the Chinese.

2 Predictions   *1½ marks for each answer*

(1) The Government is bound to be defeated in the next election.
(2) There are likely to be a lot of tourists there.
(3) They are unlikely to go abroad again soon.
(4) He's sure to be able to walk again soon.

3 Gap-filling   *1 mark for each answer*

(1) e.g. on how well he does
(2) e.g. would discourage people from smoking
(3) e.g. you look after them properly
(4) e.g. to be considering the issue
(5) e.g. the Earth's supply of oxygen will begin to run out
(6) e.g. are sorted and sent
(7) the air (from) escaping
(8) e.g. it would keep the centre free of heavy traffic

4 Vocabulary   *1 mark for each answer*

(1) expands/melts
(2) melt
(3) set/harden
(4) stretches
(5) dissolve

5 Composition   *6 marks for each paragraph*

FINAL ACHIEVEMENT TEST

1 Multiple choice   *1 mark for each answer*

(1) (b)	(6) (c)	(11) (c)	(16) (d)
(2) (a)	(7) (d)	(12) (b)	(17) (c)
(3) (b)	(8) (d)	(13) (d)	(18) (d)
(4) (d)	(9) (b)	(14) (b)	(19) (a)
(5) (b)	(10) (d)	(15) (a)	(20) (d)

2 Sentence rewriting   *2 marks for each answer*

(1) Have you ever had your photograph taken?
(2) He warned me that he would shoot if I came any closer.
(3) The Minister seems to have been given very bad advice (by the experts).
(4) The doctor wanted to know if I had been taking the tablets he had given me.
(5) He is thought to be travelling under a false name.
(6) If I had known there wouldn't be a restaurant open, I would have brought some food.
(7) He is bound to be chosen to play for the international team.
(8) They have built a special fence to prevent / which will prevent animals (from) getting in and destroying the crops.
(9) I wish I had told them the truth.
(10) As soon as he'd repaired the car, he crashed it again.

3   Writing a letter   *2 marks for each sentence*

(1)   Monica has been away for a week now – she has gone to stay with her mother / at her mother's.
(2)   The flat seems very quiet, but I'm gradually getting used to living on my own.
(3)   Last night I decided to go and eat in a restaurant nearby.
(4)   I'd never been there before and/so I wanted to see what it was like.
(5)   I'd only just sat down when the waiter rushed across the restaurant shouting 'Peter!'.
(6)   It was Arnold Freeman, (who had been) my closest friend at school.
(7)   It took me a few seconds to recognise him.
(8)   I hadn't seen him for ten years and he had changed a lot.
(9)   We spent hours talking about what we had done / been doing since we had left school.
(10) He also served me the best (and cheapest!) meal I have / had ever had.

4   Gap-filling   *1 mark for each answer*

(1)   e.g. did it take you to sort out those books
(2)   e.g. she was in Paris
(3)   e.g. do you want to use them for
(4)   e.g. I had driven all over the world
(5)   e.g. before it finally appeared
(6)   e.g. that gets on my nerves
(7)   e.g. have only been working for
(8)   e.g. you keep to the main roads
(9)   e.g. aliens had visited this planet
(10) e.g. with keeping pets
(11) e.g. the coffee beans have been picked
(12) e.g. have asked the neighbours to come in

5   Vocabulary   *½ mark for each answer*

(1) (a) drill holes
     (b) dry your washing
     (c) pump up tyres
     (d) read about your future

(2) (a) unsociable/shy
     (b) untrustworthy/unreliable
     (c) credulous/gullible/naive
     (d) vain/self-satisfied/conceited

(3) (a) fascinated
     (b) impressive
     (c) embarrassed
     (d) confusing
     (e) depressing
(4) (These are drawings.)

6   Composition   *5 marks for each paragraph*